THE POCKET GUIDE TO
BIRDS
OF
BRITAIN & EUROPE

THE POCKET GUIDE TO
BIRDS
OF
BRITAIN AND EUROPE

MARTIN WALTERS

PARKGATE
BOOKS

First published in 1990

This edition published in 1998 by
Parkgate Books Ltd
Kiln House
210 New Kings Road
London SW6 4NZ
Great Britain

9 8 7 6 5 4 3 2 1

First published by Dragon's World Ltd in 1990 at £6.95

Editor: Trish Burgess
Design: *Ann Doolan*
Editorial Director: Pippa Rubinstein

British Library Cataloguing in Publication Date:
A catalogue record for this book is available from the British
Library.

ISBN 1 85585 359 0

Printed and bound in Italy

Contents

INTRODUCTION	6
ORGANIZATIONS	12
Divers and Grebes	13
Sea Birds	16
Herons, Bitterns, Storks & Others	19
Swans & Geese	24
Ducks	28
Birds of Prey	38
Game Birds	48
Rails & Crakes	54
Cranes & Bustards	56
Waders	58
Skuas & Gulls	74
Terns & Auks	80
Doves & Pigeons	86
Owls & Nightjar	89
Swifts, Kingfishers & Others	94
Woodpeckers & Wryneck	97
Larks, Pipits & Wagtails	100
Martins & Swallows	106
Shrikes & Waxwing	108
Dipper, Wrens & Accentors	110
Warblers	112
Flycatchers	123
Chats, Thrushes & Others	127
Tits	132
Nuthatches & Creepers	136
Snow Finch & Sparrows	137
Buntings	139
Finches	143
Starlings & Oriole	149
Crows	150
FURTHER READING	156
INDEX	157

Introduction

This new book aims to provide the non-expert reader with a handy guide to all the bird species which can commonly be seen wild in Britain, Ireland, and the rest of Europe. While some priority has been given to British and Irish birds, and to those of northern Europe, most species occurring in central and southern Europe have also been included (unless they are rare or for other reasons unlikely to be spotted).

Although most of these species breed in the area, the book also includes many which do not, but which nevertheless can be seen regularly – often in large numbers – at certain times of the year. Examples are the migratory geese and swans, and some waders, many of which nest in the Arctic tundra, but which move south for the autumn and winter to the more productive feeding grounds on the coasts of north-western Europe. Those species which do not breed in Britain or Ireland are flagged with an * after their names.

The total number of species included is 349 including similar species, 286 of which are illustrated. Usually the illustration shows the adult male in breeding plumage. Frequently it is the male which has the brightest colours; the female and juveniles often have duller, more camouflaged plumage. Camouflage helps to protect the birds from their predators, while the eye-catching breeding plumage (usually, but not always, male) has evolved under the pressure of sexual selection in courtship, involving generations of female choice.

The Descriptions

For each species, the text gives a concise description of the key **Identification** features: mainly body shape, colour and pattern of plumage and also, where appropriate, details of any characteristic or unusual behaviour as well.

This identification section is followed by a description of the **Voice** – the commonest calls or songs – another feature of great importance in identification. Often a bird cannot be seen clearly, because it may be too far away, or hiding in the undergrowth or foliage. In these cases, knowledge of the call or song is often of great help in establishing a clear identity. It is difficult to describe sounds in words, so I have used a simple phonetic system, combined with suitable descriptive words.

The next part of the entry gives notes about the **Habitat** in which the bird is typically found. Birds occupy a wide range of natural and semi-natural habitats, frequently making use of more than one type over the course of the year. From the open seas and rocky coasts, through the variety of lowland habitats, to inland rivers and lakes, right up to the inhospitable high mountains and alpine tundra, birds are a prominent feature of nature. This, in turn, means that the bird-watcher can find something of interest wherever she or he might travel. Birds, unlike most wild mammals, are mostly active in the daytime and so are much easier to spot.

Notes on the **Breeding Range** follow. Birds very often nest in one kind of habitat, but move to occupy a completely different sort of environment outside the breeding season. Many species have also managed to exploit man-made habitats. For instance, Rock Doves and Swifts now nest on buildings in towns and cities, often in preference to their natural habitat of cliffs. Montagu's Harriers are birds of heath, grassland and fen, but nest increasingly among agricultural crops, as do Great Bustards, once denizens of dry steppe country.

In this section I quote the areas of Europe in which the species normally breeds in reasonable numbers. In many cases those countries with the main populations are named. For those species which are rather rare in Britain and Ireland (or for which the British or Irish totals are a significant fraction of the European population), an indication is given of the approximate numbers of pairs breeding (based on the most up-to-date assessments).

The section entitled **Movements** explains whether the species is resident (remains throughout the year), or is a summer or winter visitor, or passage migrant. Note that the same species can fall into more than one of these categories, often behaving differently in different parts of its geographical range.

Few species are purely resident, even those which can be seen at all times of the year. This apparent paradox is because part of the population only may migrate. Many common 'residents', such as Great Tit and Robin, behave in this way. Populations of many others, such as Starling, Snipe and Curlew, receive a large winter influx by migration.

Many geese, ducks and waders make regular migrations from their northern breeding grounds to the ice-free parts of northwestern Europe. Birds put on extra fat before migration, and may then fly non-stop to their wintering grounds, often at night. The thin 'seep' flight-call of migrating Redwings at night is a familiar sound of late autumn.

Under **Similar Species**, I mention birds which resemble the main species, but which are either less common or are less likely to be spotted.

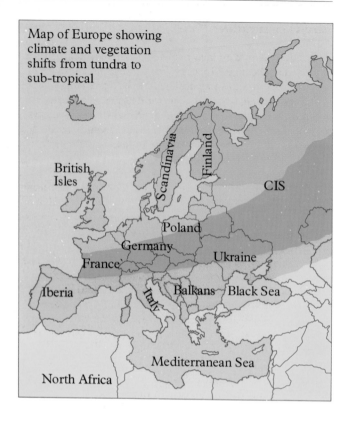

Map of Europe showing climate and vegetation shifts from tundra to sub-tropical

British Isles

Scandinavia

Finland

CIS

Poland

Germany

France

Ukraine

Iberia

Italy

Balkans

Black Sea

Mediterranean Sea

North Africa

The order of the species entries is systematic and traditional, in line with most bird guides. This order aims to treat the families in a sequence which reflects their evolutionary relationships (although these relationships are not always known, and are increasingly being questioned by current genetic research).

The advantage of the sequence is that similar birds are dealt with close together in the book, which greatly assists in making comparisons. In addition, all the species belonging to the same family (for example the Thrush Family or the Heron Family) appear together in the same section. Where possible, I have tried to arrange the order so that similar species appear on the same spread, again as an aid to identification.

Bird Conservation

Bird conservation is an important activity, not just for the sake of particular endangered species, but because birds provide us with an index of the overall health of our environment.

If birds decline, we should look for the reasons and then try to put matters right. The populations of many of Europe's birds of prey for example have declined in recent decades, partly due to pesticide poisoning, partly because of hunting, and partly through habitat destruction.

Thankfully, many species (such as Sparrowhawk and Peregrine) are now recovering, following the banning of certain toxic chemicals and a generally improved awareness of all of these threats. Often, those factors responsible for the decline in bird numbers will in turn be harmful to ourselves, so it is not just for the birds' sake that we should be concerned.

The emphasis in bird conservation has shifted in recent years away from schemes to protect individual species (although these are still worthwhile in some cases) to efforts to protect their habitats. In general, if the habitat is healthy, then varied populations of interesting birds will thrive, as will other associated animals, and the plants upon which they all depend.

One case-history from many possible conservation stories exemplifies the success of this habitat-led approach. Marsh Harriers are relatively rare breeders in Britain, with their stronghold in the marshes of eastern England. This species almost became extinct in the early 1970s, but numbers have now built up to about one hundred pairs, largely because large reed bed reserves have been maintained around the Suffolk and Norfolk coasts. However, not all stories are as successful.

Contrast this with the status of the Bittern, that strange, owl-coloured, shy heron of the reeds. Its habitat requirements appear similar to those of the Marsh Harrier, but despite plenty of apparently suitable habitats, numbers continue to decline over most of Europe (with the exception of Denmark, Finland and Estonia which report a slight increase). In Britain, the Bittern is clinging on with about fifteen breeding pairs, mainly in coastal Norfolk and Suffolk. Bitterns are highly susceptible to disturbance from anglers and other river users, and also sensitive to pollution.

Bird Anatomy and Key Features

While technical terms have been kept to a minimum, some are needed to refer to parts of the bird's anatomy mentioned in the species accounts. The simplified diagram shows the main parts of a typical bird.

Variations in the colouring and patterns created by the feathers endow birds with a powerful method of signalling to each other, and, incidentally, also make our task of identifying the species that much easier. Many birds, such as female ducks, owls and woodcock, have highly camouflaged plumage, enabling them to escape detection when at rest, or at the nest. Even those species which may have quite bold patterns or conspicuous plumage, can often be hard to spot when in their normal habitat. Thus a Grey Heron, when seen at close quarters, has quite bold markings, but often blends well into its surroundings at the water's edge.

A bird's head often bears distinctive markings. There may be an obvious eye-stripe, just above or through the eye, or a stripe along the crown. Some birds have a crest on top of their head, or a dark cap. Other common head markings include a moustache, or an obvious mask-like patch.

The throat and breast often have prominent marks too. These may be patches of contrasting colours, spots or bars. Very often birds are dark above, but pale or white on the belly, flank and under their wings. This probably helps give them protection, by making them harder to spot from above (normally against a dark background) and from below (normally against the paler back lighting of the sky).

The unfurling of wings and tail allow birds to hide prominent signal markings when at rest. Wings, tail and rump often have contrasting patterns or colours which only become obvious during flight. The wings may or may not have a bar (frequently white), and in similar species this can be used as a reliable identification character.

Legs vary enormously in length, usually connected with the bird's feeding method. Waders and herons have long legs, whilst many perching birds have short legs. Toes may be long and thin, rough, end in sturdy claws, be lobed or fully webbed. Again, here we see a clear relationship with their preferred feeding method or usual habitat.

Note that very often the plumage varies markedly from season to season. The bright breeding plumage (usually the male) may change to a drabber pattern (often more like the female) during autumn and winter, and juvenile birds may differ again, but often resemble the winter male or female. Illustration of all these plumage variations is however beyond the scope of this guide, and the reader should consult more detailed reference books for this information.

Birds have acute vision, and many species have quite large eyes. Eyes vary in colour (according to the species) from brown and grey, to bright yellow, or even red. The skin around the eye may also be brightly coloured, to create an obvious eye-ring.

The experienced bird-watcher uses a combination of cues, often subconsciously, when making an identification and, after years of practice, integration of features such as size, shape, plumage patterns, behaviour and calls becomes second nature.

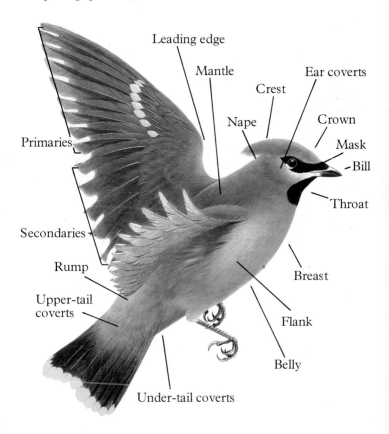

Identifying Birds in the Field

Many aspects of a bird offer important clues to their identity.
These may include the general shape, the patterns and colour
of plumage, the call, and also species-typical behaviour. You
also learn to expect certain species to show up in particular
places, and this does help in identification. Of course you must
keep an open mind so as not to miss spotting an unusual
visitor, or a bird straying outside its normal environment (as
often happens during migration).

Birds vary as to how often they call, and also in the variety
of calls uttered. Some, such as gulls and terns at their breeding
sites, keep up an almost constant clamour, while other species,
for example Golden Eagle, are normally silent. Most birds
make contact calls and alarm calls in addition to their often
elaborate courtship songs. The song, normally given by the
male, serves both to define the bounds of his territory and to
alert the female to his presence. Species which tend to move
around in flocks often have simple contact calls which they use
to keep in touch with each other. Alarm calls, typically given
near the nest, warn of danger. These are often short and sharp;
easy to hear but sometimes difficult for people and predators to
locate. Flight calls are contact calls given in flight – like the
musical honking of swans or the piping calls of waders.

Organizations

Without the efforts of the conservation organizations and
individuals, there would be fewer bird species to spot and an
even more rapid rate of disappearance of suitable habitats.
They need all the support we can give. You can do your bit
towards helping to conserve birds and their habitats by joining
one of the following organizations:

Royal Society for the Protection of Birds (RSPB)
The Lodge, Sandy, Beds SG19 2DL

The British Trust for Ornithology (BTO)
National Centre for Ornithology, The Nunnery,
Thetford, Norfolk IP24 2PU

Scottish Ornithologists' Club
21 Regent Terrace, Edinburgh, EH7 5BT

BirdLife International (formerly ICBP) is the major body
which co-ordinates international bird conservation. This is a
global conservation federation with a worldwide network of
partners. It seeks to conserve bird species and their habitats
throughout the world. Join their **World Bird Club** by writing
to Wellbrook Court, Girton Road, Cambridge, CB3 0NA.

Black-throated Diver

Gavia arctica 58–68 cm (23–27 ins)

Identification Duck-like, with rather snake-like head. Bill held straight, head upright. In breeding plumage, has grey head, black throat and striped neck. Back with striking black and white markings. In winter, uniform dark above, pale underneath, with clear border on head and neck; bill black. Juveniles in winter rather paler.

Voice Seldom heard in winter; long drawn-out wail, also meowing call when disturbed.

Habitat Large lakes in summer. In winter, usually coastal seas.

Breeding range Northern Europe, mainly Scandinavia and Scotland.

Movements Winters on North Sea and Baltic, more rarely on large inland lakes.

Similar species GREAT NORTHERN DIVER*, *Gavia immer*, is larger, with heavier bill and (in summer) black head. Seen mainly in winter on coasts of north-western Europe.

Red-throated Diver

Gavia stellata 53–58 cm (21–23 ins)

Identification Somewhat smaller than Black-throated Diver, with slimmer head, neck and bill (latter slightly upturned). Head normally tilted upwards. In breeding plumage, has red-brown patch on neck, looking black from a distance. In winter, very like Black-throated, but back lighter. Less distinct border between dark and pale colours on head and neck.

Voice Wailing on breeding grounds; occasional ringing 'ah-oo-ah' in winter, goose-like flight-call.

Habitat Small lakes in moorland and tundra; coastal in winter.

Breeding range Iceland, Scandinavia, northern Britain.

Movements Winters mostly on North Sea and Baltic coasts; rare but regular on inland lakes, reservoirs and larger rivers.

* denotes species not breeding regularly in Britain and Ireland

Great Crested Grebe
Podiceps cristata 45–51 cm (18–20 ins)

Identification Our largest grebe. Striking head and neck feathers form a ruff in breeding season. In winter, has dark cap, white cheeks and front of neck and a clear white stripe above eye. Juveniles have striped head and neck. Swims deep in water.

Voice Raw 'gruck-gruck', hoarse 'rah-rah', mostly in spring.

Habitat Large lakes with reedy margins, sometimes on small lakes or reservoirs.

Breeding range Common over much of Europe, except Scotland and Scandinavia.

Movements In winter, often in flocks on large lakes and rivers, and coastal seas.

Red-necked Grebe★
Podiceps grisegena 40–46 cm (16–18 ins)

Identification More compact than Great Crested Grebe, with shorter, thicker neck. In breeding plumage, has rusty-red neck, white cheeks and throat and a black bill, yellow towards base. In winter, plumage very like Great Crested, but with greyer neck and lacking the white stripe over the eye.

Voice A loud, whinnying display call; sharp alarm call 'eck-eck-eck'. Usually silent in winter.

Habitat Breeds on reedy, shallower lakes.

Breeding range Mainly eastern Europe to Denmark and northern Germany.

Movements In winter, on lakes and coastal seas, occasionally on rivers.

Little Grebe (Dabchick)
Tachybaptus ruficollis 25–29 cm (10–11 ins)

Identification Our smallest grebe, dumpy and short-necked. In breeding plumage, has chestnut brown head and sides of neck, and an obvious bright spot at base of bill. In winter, uniform grey-brown, somewhat lighter on flanks.

Voice Long, vibrating trill, mainly in spring; also a high-pitched 'bi-ib'.

Habitat Well vegetated ponds and small lakes, slow rivers.

Breeding range Most of Europe, except the north.

Movements In winter, often in small flocks on rivers, lakes and ponds.

Slavonian Grebe
Podiceps auritus 31–36 cm (12–14 ins)

Identification Small, slimmer and somewhat longer-necked than Little Grebe. In summer has black head, with golden 'horns', neck and underparts rusty red. In winter, grey with white neck and lower face, and black cap.

Voice Trills and squeals on breeding ground.

Habitat Breeds on shallow lakes.

Breeding range Northern Europe (Iceland, Norway, Sweden, Finland); small population in Scotland (about seventy-five pairs).

Movements Regular but rare winter visitor to Britain and Ireland, mainly to coasts and estuaries.

Similar species BLACK-NECKED GREBE, *Podiceps nigricollis*, is slightly smaller, with upturned bill. In winter, neck and face are dusky grey. In summer, mainly black, with rusty flanks, and golden fan of feathers behind eyes. In Britain and Ireland breeds locally, in small numbers (about thirty pairs).

Storm Petrel
Hydrobates pelagicus 14–16 cm (5–6 ins)

Identification Very small, dark sea bird with obvious white rump. Flight fluttery, dipping to surface sometimes with legs dangling. Pale wing-bar, most obvious on underside.
Voice Strange purring and squeaking at breeding colonies.
Habitat Open sea, except when breeding at offshore islands.
Breeding range Coasts and islands of Iceland, western Britain and Ireland, France and Mediterranean.
Movements Outside breeding season ranges widely over open sea.

Manx Shearwater
Puffinus puffinus
30–38 cm (12–15 ins)

Identification Black and white sea bird with long, narrow, stiffly-held wings. Glides low over the waves; wing-beats shallow, rapid and intermittent.
Voice Weird screaming and wailing at breeding colonies.
Habitat Oceanic, except when breeding. Feeds in flocks offshore.
Breeding range Coasts and islands of Iceland, western Britain and Ireland, France and Mediterranean.
Movements Ranges widely over open sea outside breeding season.

Fulmar

Fulmarus glacialis 44–50 cm (17–20 ins)

Identification Gull-like, but plumper, with thicker head and neck. Bill short and broad. Glides on stiffly held wings with occasional wing-beats.
Voice Rasping calls and also a softer flight-call.
Habitat Breeds in colonies on cliffs, rocky coasts and islands. Outside breeding season often at sea far from coasts.
Breeding range Around coasts of northern Europe, from Iceland and Norway, Britain and Ireland, south to northern France.
Movements Atlantic and North Sea, occasionally in Baltic.

Gannet

Morus bassanus 86–96 cm (34–38 ins)

Identification Large, graceful black and white (adult) sea bird with pointed head and tail, and long, rather narrow, black-tipped wings. Juveniles brown, gradually turning whiter over five years. Glides and soars, occasionally plunge-diving for fish.

Voice Barking and growling at breeding site.
Habitat Open sea. Breeds in often huge colonies on inaccessible rocky islands.
Breeding range North-western Europe. Britain and Ireland have 70 per cent of total world population (about 185,000 pairs).
Movements Ranges widely outside breeding season, south to western Mediterranean.

Cormorant

Phalacrocorax carbo 85–90 cm (33–35 ins)

Identification Mainly black water bird with white chin and cheeks, and long, hooked bill. White patch on thigh in breeding season. Juveniles brownish, with whitish underside. Swims low in water, like divers. Often perches with wings spread out.

Voice Raw, grating gurgling and crowing, usually only heard on breeding ground.

Habitat Breeds in colonies on rocky coasts, also inland, usually on islands in large lakes, often in tall trees.

Breeding range Britain, Ireland, Holland, northern Germany and Poland.

Movements Regular on larger lakes in winter, and in shallow coastal waters.

Shag

Phalacrocorax aristotelis
72–80 cm (28–31 ins)

Identification Similar to Cormorant, but smaller and more strictly coastal. Black plumage with a greenish tinge; upturned crest in breeding season.

Voice Grunts and hisses at breeding site.

Habitat Breeds in colonies on rocky coasts and cliff-bases.

Breeding range In Britain and Ireland, more northern and western than Cormorant.

However has wider range in Europe, from Iceland to Iberia, Corsica, Sardinia and east coast of Adriatic Sea.

Movements Mainly resident, but is sometimes seen inland in winter.

Grey Heron

Ardea cinerea 90–100 cm (35–39 ins)

Identification Commonest and largest
heron. Long neck and legs; long, pointed,
yellowish bill. Plumage mainly grey;
black stripe above eye, continued as two
long drooping feathers. Young birds
lack eye-stripe and plume feathers.
Flies slowly, with heavy wing-beats
and S-shaped neck, legs outstretched
behind.
Voice Flight-call a raw, hollow croak.
Habitat Breeds in colonies in tall trees,
occasionally in reed beds. Feeds in shallow
water of ponds, rivers, lakes, salt marshes,
estuaries and rocky coasts. Also hunts frogs
and small rodents in damp fields.
Breeding range Widespread in Europe, except far north and
east. Local in Spain and Portugal. About 1,500 pairs in Britain
and Ireland. High mortality in hard winters.
Movements Mainly resident; migrates from cold winter areas.

Purple Heron★

Ardea purpurea
75–85 cm (30–33 ins)

Identification Slimmer and
longer-necked than Grey Heron;
plumage very dark, especially in
flight. Often holds neck in snake-
like curve (neck looks angular in
flight). Juveniles paler, lacking black head
and neck markings; easily confused with
Grey Heron from a distance.
Voice Flight-call rather higher pitched
than Grey Heron.
Habitat Large reed beds, and marshy
areas with thick scrub.
Breeding range Mainly southern Europe, but north to Holland.
Rare and irregular breeding, mostly in small, short-lived colonies.
Larger colonies in Holland and Austria/Hungary Neusiedlersee.
Movements Summer visitor.

Bittern
Botaurus stellaris 70–80 cm (28–31 ins)

Identification A squat, brown heron, with
relatively short neck. Plumage reed-coloured
(for camouflage), legs and toes green. Flight
owl-like, with head stretched out in short flight,
tucked in for longer flight. Clambers slowly among
reeds. Stands motionless with head erect when
disturbed, often for long periods.
Voice Foghorn-like booming during breeding
season; flight-call a raw croak.
Habitat Breeds in large reed beds near lakes,
marshes and bogs.
Breeding range Scattered and patchy in Europe, absent from
north. Rare and decreasing over most of range. British
population now down to about fifteen pairs.
Movements Mainly resident in west, summer visitor in east.

Little Bittern★
Ixobrychus minutus 33–38 cm (13–15 ins)

Identification Europe's smallest heron. Male has dark cap
and upper side. Female less contrasted, streaked on neck,
breast and flanks. Pale wings obvious in flight, especially male.
Voice Flight-call a short, raw croak. Male also has low,
repeated bark in breeding season. Flies low over reeds, with
rapid wing-beats, quickly diving down into fresh cover.
Habitat Thick reed beds on lakes,
damp riverside willow scrub,
marshes and flood-plain woods.
Breeding range Central and southern
Europe. Local, and mostly more common
in the east of range. Range reduced by
habitat destruction.
Movements Summer visitor.
Similar species NIGHT HERON★, *Nycticorax
nycticorax*, is larger, and grey and black
(juvenile brown). It is mainly active at dawn
and dusk. Rare in northern and central Europe,
with a few small colonies in Holland and
southern Germany; somewhat more common in
Hungary, the Czech Republic and Slovakia.

Little Egret*
Egretta garzetta
50–56 cm (20–22 ins)

Identification White with black bill, black
legs and yellow feet. Long plumes on head
and shoulders in breeding season, raised
during displays. In flight, has relatively
rapid wing-beat, and rounded wings.
Yellow feet most visible in flight.
Voice Various raucous gurgling and snoring noises at nest.
Habitat Breeds in colonies in large wetlands with bushes and
trees, but also in rice fields. Runs rapidly in shallow water,
stabbing to left and right for small fish, frogs and aquatic insects.
Breeding range Mainly southern Europe. Rare breeder in
Czechoslovakia and Hungary; regular in summer at
Neusiedlersee (Austria and Hungary).
Movements Summer visitor (resident in southern Spain).
Similar species GREAT WHITE EGRET*, *Casmerodius albus*,
is larger, with dark legs and feet. Regular breeder on
Neusiedlersee. Otherwise rare visitor to suitable sites.

Cattle Egret*
Bubulcus ibis 48–53 cm (19–21 ins)

Identification Smaller and shorter-necked than Little Egret,
with buff colouration on breast, back and head in breeding
season. Legs and feet dark. Distinct jowl under lower mandible.
Often associates with livestock.

Voice Bubbling and croaking at breeding
site.
Habitat Marshes, farmland and open
fields.
Breeding range Southern Spain and
Portugal, north to south of France.
Movements Resident and partial migrant.
Similar species SQUACCO HERON*, *Ardeola
ralloides*, is smaller, and brownish all over,
except for white wings and rump.
Local summer visitor to reed
beds and marshes of southern
and eastern Europe.

White Stork*

Ciconia ciconia 95–105 cm (37–41 ins)

Identification Very large and white with black flight feathers; long, red bill and legs. Juveniles have much paler bill and legs. Flies and soars with neck outstretched, unlike herons.
Voice Noisy bill-clapping during breeding displays. Occasional hissing.
Habitat Damp meadows and fields in open lowland. Breeds mainly on buildings and chimneys, often on a specially-provided wheel. Sometimes nests in trees in river-valley woodland.
Breeding range Mainly north-eastern central Europe. Also south-western Spain and Portugal. In western Europe has been decreasing markedly for decades, mainly because of habitat destruction, collisions with power-lines and shooting in winter quarters.
Movements Summer visitor. Resident in southern Iberia.

Black Stork*

Ciconia nigra 90–100 cm (35–39 ins)

Identification Similar size to White Stork, but mainly black plumage, with greenish and purple sheen. Only belly and under tail coverts white. Juveniles grey-brown, with greenish bill and legs. Often soars for long periods at a great height.
Voice Melodious flight-call when soaring; various grating and musical noises at nest, also bill-clapping.
Habitat Mainly woodland. Breeds in old undisturbed mixed forest near rivers, pools, ponds and wet meadows. Feeds exclusively in shallow water. Builds large stick nest in an old tree.
Breeding range Eastern Europe from Poland to Greece. Also in central and southern Iberia. Severely reduced by habitat destruction and afforestation, but evidence of slow recovery.
Movements Summer visitor in east, resident in Iberia.

Spoonbill★
Platalea leucorodia 78–85 cm (31–33 ins)

Identification Long spoon-shaped bill with yellow tip. White plumage with yellow-ochre chin. In breeding season, has crest behind head and yellowish breast-band. Juveniles lack crest, yellow chin spot and breast-band, and wings have dark tips. In flight, head and neck outstretched; neck sagging slightly. Stands in water and sieves small animals by swishing bill from side to side. Flocks often fly in long lines or in V-formation.
Voice Nasal grunting and wailing sounds at nest.
Habitat Marshy areas, with reed beds and shallow water.
Breeding range Rare breeding bird in Holland, Austria, Hungary and Greece. Also south-western Spain.
Movements Summer visitor (resident in Spain). Often at coasts outside breeding season.

Greater Flamingo★
Phoenicopterus ruber
125–145 cm (49–57 ins)

Identification Long pink legs, curved neck and heavy, bent beak. Wings have pink leading edge and black trailing edge. Neck and legs held stretched out and sagging below body-line in flight. Juvenile dingy grey-brown.
Voice Goose-like honking and gabbling, mainly in flight.
Habitat Saline lagoons, lakes, mud-flats.
Breeding range Colonies in southern France (Camargue) and southern Spain (Coto Donana and elsewhere).
Movements Resident. French population mainly summer visitors.

Mute Swan
Cygnus olor
145–160 cm (57–63 ins)

Identification Largest
and heaviest water bird.
Pure white plumage, bill
reddish with black base; obvious knob on bill, more developed
in male, especially in spring. Juveniles grey-brown; bill grey,
without knob. Swims with neck held in S-shaped curve. Flies
with powerful wing-beats, with neck stretched out. Wings make
distinct swishing sound.
Voice Fairly silent; occasional hissing in defence.
Habitat Lakes, gravel pits and ponds, even in urban areas. In
winter, often in large numbers on lakes. Breeds in lakes with
rich vegetation and reedy banks; also banks of slow rivers and
near the coast. Makes large nest of old reeds and other plant
material. Semi-domesticated in many areas.
Breeding range North-western Europe, east to Baltic. Also
northern Greece, Romania.
Movements Partial migrant.

Whooper Swan
Cygnus cygnus 145–160 cm (57–63 ins)

Identification As large as Mute Swan but slimmer. Bill has
yellow wedge-shaped patch and lacks knob at base. Neck held
straight. Juveniles greyer than young Mute, bill flesh-coloured
with darker tip. Flocks often fly in formation.
Voice Calls frequently; swimming flocks have goose-like nasal
calls; loud trumpeting calls before and during migration.
Habitat Breeds in bogs and around tundra lakes.
Breeding range Iceland and Fennoscandia, south to Baltic
area. About five pairs breed each year in Britain and Ireland.
Movements Regular winter visitor in large flocks to
North Sea and Baltic coasts, as well as to lakes,
flooded rivers. Large numbers visit Ireland
and Britain (mainly from Iceland).
Similar species BEWICK'S
SWAN*, *Cygnus columbianus*,
is smaller with variable
yellow/orange bill patch. Regular
winter visitor to north-western Europe
from Siberian breeding ground.

Canada Goose
Branta canadensis 55–100 cm (22–39 ins)

Identification Very large goose (though the species is variable, with some small races) with long, black neck. Head black and white; tail, bill and feet black. Flocks often fly in V-formation.

Voice Flight-call a nasal trumpeting, accented on the second syllable.

Habitat Reservoirs, lakes, fish ponds and ornamental lakes in parks. Introduced from North America; originally bred on marshy lakes and river banks, right up into tundra region.

Breeding range British Isles. Also locally in Scandinavia.

Movements Resident and partial migrant. Mainly partial migrant to Germany and Holland. Swedish population winters on German North Sea coast.

Barnacle Goose★
Branta leucopsis 58–68 cm (23–27 ins)

Identification Medium-sized goose with small, black bill. From distance looks black above, white below. White face contrasts with black neck. First year juvenile has grey-white face, dark brown neck. Flocks usually unstructured in flight.

Voice Flight-call a soft puppy-like yapping.

Habitat Winters on salt marshes, mud flats and coastal pasture.

Breeding range Mainly on cliffs above river valleys or fjords in Greenland, Spitzbergen and northern Russia.

Movements Regular winter visitor to Scotland, Ireland, and to south-eastern North Sea.

Brent Goose★
Branta bernicla 55–60 cm (22–24 ins)

Identification Small, dark, rather duck-like goose with black bill and legs. White 'stern' contrasts with rest of plumage. Two races visit Europe: a pale-bellied and a (commoner) dark-bellied form. Irish birds are mainly pale-bellied while those visiting southern England and continental Europe are mostly dark-bellied. Usually forms large, loose flocks. Flight rapid.
Voice Deep nasal 'rott-rott-rott' or guttural 'rronk' when disturbed; flight-call short hard 'ack' mixed with quieter, higher-pitched calls.
Habitat Winters on mud flats and coastal fields. Numbers drastically reduced by hunting and decline in eelgrass beds.
Breeding range In colonies near lakes in coastal Arctic tundra.
Movements Autumn and winter visitor to coasts of north-western Europe.

White-fronted Goose★
Anser albifrons
65–76 cm (26–30 ins)

Identification Medium-sized goose, with black horizontal barring on belly. Forehead white. Bill long and pink in Russian race; orange-yellow in Greenland race. Juveniles lack black belly markings and white patch, bill has darker tip.
Voice High-pitched rapid 'kwi-kwi-kwi', or 'keowlyow'.
Habitat Feeds on coastal meadows and salt marshes by day, spending night on the water.
Breeding range Tundra of northern Russia and Greenland.
Movements Winter visitor in flocks to British Isles, notably Ireland, western Scotland (Greenland race). Also North Sea and Channel coasts (mainly Russian race).
Similar species LESSER WHITE-FRONTED GOOSE★, *Anser erythropus*, is smaller and shorter necked, with rounder head and shorter bill. White patch extends above eye, which has a characteristic yellow ring. Flight very agile. Rare, yet regular winter visitor to British Isles. Normally winters in Balkans.

Pink-footed Goose★

Anser brachyrhynchus
61–76 cm (24–30 ins)

Identification A rather small,
compact, grey goose, showing
pale leading edge to wing
in flight (like Greylag).
Head is dark, and white
upper tail shows clearly in flight. Legs
pink; bill small and pink, dark at base.
Voice Very vocal. Musical calls include
'unk-unk' and higher-pitched 'wink-wink'.
Habitat Breeds on rocky sites and tundra (Iceland).
Winters on pasture, stubble fields and salt marsh.
Breeding range Iceland.
Movements Winters in large flocks to traditional sites in
northern Britain (notably Scotland and Lancashire), and south-
eastern Ireland. Also to south-eastern coasts, usually only after
hard weather, and to southern coasts of North Sea.
Similar species BEAN GOOSE★, *Anser fabalis*, is larger and has
orange bill and feet. Wings uniformly dark. Winters around
coasts of Europe. In Britain, mainly south-western Scotland
(Solway) and East Anglia (small numbers). Vagrant to Ireland.

Greylag Goose

Anser anser
76–89 cm (30–35 ins)

Identification Largest of the
grey geese, and the ancestor of the
farmyard goose. Bill orange-yellow
(western race) or flesh-coloured (eastern
race), with intermediates. Feet flesh-pink, grey in juveniles. In
flight, shows clear, silver-grey leading edge to the broad wings.
Voice Rather vocal: a nasal 'ga-ga-ga', 'ang-ang-ang',
or similar.
Habitat Breeds on large inland lakes with thick fringing
vegetation or in bogs. Winters on coastal marshes and fields.
Breeding range Iceland and Scandinavia and patchily from
Britain to eastern and south-eastern Europe. In Britain and
Ireland, total population about 22,000 pairs, a large proportion
(especially in the south) not of truly wild origin.
Movements Resident and partial migrant.

Shelduck
Tadorna tadorna
58–64 cm (23–25 ins)

Identification Large goose-sized
duck, looking black and white in
distance. Broad chestnut band
around body at chest region. Male
has knob at base of bill. Juveniles
mostly grey-brown above, whitish
below, with light grey bill and feet. Flies with relatively slow
wing-beats, in lines or wedge formation.
Voice Male has piping 'tyu-tyu-tyu-tyu' and a trill; female calls
much deeper 'ga-ga-ga-ga' or 'ark'.
Habitat: Muddy and sandy coasts, and coastal lakes. Nests in
holes and rabbit burrows.
Breeding range Coasts of north-western Europe, and
patchily in Mediterranean. Common breeding bird of North
Sea and Baltic.
Movements Resident and partial migrant (Scandinavian
populations are summer visitors).

Wigeon
Anas penelope 43–48 cm (17–19 ins)

Identification Medium-sized duck with
tucked-in head, high forehead and
short bill. Breeding male has
chestnut head with golden crown
stripe; female similar to Mallard
female, but slimmer, with rusty
brown plumage and more pointed
tail. In flight, note the long wings and white
belly, also large white wing patches of male. Often forms large
flocks in winter.
Voice Male whistling 'whee-oo', with accent on first syllable;
female rattling 'rrarr'.
Habitat Lakes and muddy shores, estuaries.
Breeding range Breeds on lakes, bogs and river deltas in
northern Europe (mainly Iceland and Scandinavia). In Britain
and Ireland, about 450 pairs, mainly in the north.
Movements Regular winter visitor to North Sea, southern
Baltic, and other coasts.

Teal

Anas crecca 34–38 cm (13–15 ins)

Identification Our smallest duck, with rapid, wader-like flight. Breeding male has chestnut and green head, and yellow triangle (bordered black) at side of tail. Female has yellow-brown spots and dark grey bill. Both sexes show white wing-bar and green speculum in flight.
Voice Male melodious 'krick', often in flight; female has a higher-pitched quack.
Habitat Breeds on lakes with thick bank vegetation.
Breeding range Widespread in northern and eastern Europe, rarer further south. About

3,000 pairs in Britain and Ireland.
Movements Northern breeders move south for winter. More common outside breeding season, especially on flooded meadows and marshland.

Garganey

Anas querquedula 37–40 cm (15–16 ins)

Identification Slightly larger yet slimmer than Teal. Breeding male has broad white eye-stripe reaching to back of head. Female like Teal, but with rather striped face pattern. Male in eclipse like female, but with blue-grey front of wing. Flight not as rapid as Teal.
Voice Breeding male has dry 'klerreb'; female has high-pitched, nasal quack.
Habitat Breeds on shallow water or marsh with rich vegetation. Outside breeding season on lakes, flooded meadows and marshes.
Breeding range In Britain and Ireland, rare breeding bird (about fifty pairs).
Movements Summer visitor to much of Europe (but absent from most of north-western and southern Europe). Winters in Africa.

Mallard
Anas platyrhynchos 55–62 cm (22–24 ins)

Identification Most well known duck, and
ancestor of domestic duck breeds. Breeding
male has shiny green head with yellow
bill, reddish brown breast and curly
black central tail feathers.
Female brown and speckled.
Voice Displaying males have
a quiet 'yeeb' and a thin,
high-pitched whistle;
females the well known quack, 'waak-wak-wak-wak-wak'.
Habitat Still or slow-flowing water. Common as a feral
bird in parks.
Breeding range Whole of Europe.
Movements Resident over most of Europe, except far
north, where its is a summer visitor.

Gadwall
Anas strepera 48–54 cm (19–21 ins)

Identification Mallard-like but slightly smaller and slimmer,
with steeper forehead. Male relatively drab, with obvious black
'stern'. In flight, both sexes show white belly and white
speculum. Female has yellow-orange edges to bill.
Voice Male has nasal 'arp' call, and whistle; female has
a Mallard-like quack 'kaak-kaak-kak-kak-kak',
in diminuendo.
Habitat Breeds on freshwater lakes with
rich vegetation, and on slow rivers.
Breeding range Patchy
distribution over much of
Europe, except the north.
About 800 pairs in Britain and
Ireland, mainly in south-east.
Movements Resident and partial
migrant. Winter numbers swelled by
migrants from further north.

Shoveler

Anas clypeata
47–53 cm (18–21 ins)

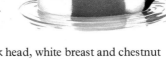

Identification Squatter
than Mallard, with more
pointed wings and long,
broad bill. Male has dark head, white breast and chestnut
belly and flanks. Female rather like Mallard, but has
pale blue forewing.
Voice Usually rather silent. Male has a deep 'tuk-tuk';
female a two-syllable quack.
Habitat Breeds on shallow lakes, bordered by rushes, sedges
or reeds, and in marshy areas with open water. Outside
breeding season also at coast.
Breeding range Scattered, mainly northern and eastern
Europe. In Britain and Ireland about 1,500 pairs.
Movements Resident in milder areas; summer visitor
elsewhere. Winter numbers swelled by migrants from
further north.

Pintail

Anas acuta 55–65 cm (22–26 ins)

Identification Slimmer than Mallard. Male has chestnut head,
grey body and long, pointed tail feathers. Female similar to
Mallard, but has more pointed tail and smaller, grey bill.
Eclipse male very similar to female, but darker above. In flight
(rapid), note long, pointed wings, slim body, long neck and
white-edged speculum.
Voice Breeding call of male a low whistle; female a grating
quack.
Habitat Breeds
mainly on shallow
lakes in northern
coniferous forest or
tundra. Outside breeding
season, mainly on the coast,
or flooded wash land.
Breeding range Mainly northern and north-eastern Europe.
Rare breeder in Britain and Ireland (about fifty pairs).
Movements Summer visitor to breeding grounds. Winter
visitor further south (mainly coastal areas).

Pochard

Aythya ferina 44–48 cm (17–19 ins)

Identification Plump, compact duck with domed head and steep forehead. Male has contrasting silver-grey back and flanks, black chest and tail, and chestnut-brown head. Female brown, with blackish bill and pale eye-ring.

Voice Rather silent. Breeding male has low nasal whistle; female a raw 'cherr-cherr'.

Habitat Breeds on rich freshwater lakes with large open areas and reeds. Outside breeding season on large lakes, reservoirs, ponds and slow-flowing rivers, often in large flocks. Sometimes tame in parks and on lakes.

Breeding range Widespread breeding bird, but rather patchy distribution. Population in Britain and Ireland about 450 pairs.

Movements Resident and partial migrant. Summer visitor to north and east of range. Numbers in Britain and Ireland swelled in winter by migrants.

Red-crested Pochard★

Netta rufina 53–59 cm (21–23 ins)

Identification Large, thick-headed diving duck, sitting rather high in the water. Breeding male has chestnut head (crown paler) and bright red bill. Female is uniform grey-brown with pale grey cheeks (see also female Common Scoter).

Voice Breeding male loud 'bait' or slow, nasal 'geng'; female a harsh 'kurr'.

Habitat Reedy lakes, mainly in drier regions.

Breeding range Only a few places in Europe, mainly in southern Spain and Camargue (France), but also in Holland, Denmark, and southern central Europe (Lake Constance and Bavaria). Sometimes escapes from collections.

Movements Summer visitor, but resident in southern Spain and southern France.

Tufted Duck
Aythya fuligula 41–45 cm (16–18 ins)

Identification Small, compact
diving duck. In flight, shows
white wing bar. Male black with
white flanks and long plume on
back of head (which has purple
sheen). Female dark brown, with head plume very short or
absent, and sometimes with white spot at base of bill. Often
forms large winter flocks.
Voice Breeding male has guttural 'gee-gee-gee'; female a
grating 'kreck-kreck'.
Habitat Lakes and reservoirs.
Breeding range Relatively common breeding bird, sometimes
in urban areas. In Britain and Ireland, about 10,000 pairs.
Movements Resident and partial migrant. Summer visitor to
northern Europe. Numbers in Britain and Ireland swelled in
winter by migrants.

Scaup★
Aythya marila 46–50 cm (18–20 ins)

Identification Larger than Tufted Duck, without plume.
Head larger and more rounded, bill wider. Male has green-
black head, pale grey speckled back and white flanks. In eclipse
less contrast, with brown head and greyish white flanks. Female
similar to Tufted, but has broad white spot at base of bill.
Voice Seldom heard. Breeding male has soft courtship calls;
female a deep, raw 'karr'.
Habitat Breeds in northern Europe at pools and lakes in the
birch and willow tundra, and at coasts. In winter, moves in
large flocks mainly to coasts and coastal lakes.
Breeding range Iceland, Scandinavia and
Finland. Occasionally Britain and Ireland.
Movements Summer visitor to
breeding grounds. Winter
visitor mainly to coasts of
north-western Europe.
In Britain and Ireland,
most common in north.

Eider

Somateria mollissima
55–60 cm (22–24 ins)

Identification Large sea-
duck, heavier than Mallard,
but more compact and shorter-
necked. Breeding male mainly
black and white. First-year males dark with partially white
feathers, giving 'dappled' pattern. Female brownish with darker
stripes. Very sociable; often fly low over water in long,
straggling flocks.
Voice Breeding male has a crooning 'ohuuo' or 'hu-huo';
female a raw 'korr'.
Habitat Breeds on coasts and nearby islands; outside breeding
season in shallow bays and estuaries.
Breeding range Coasts of Iceland, Scandinavia, northern
Britain and Ireland (about 32,000 pairs).
Movements Summer visitor in breeding range. Winters
mainly on adjacent coastal waters, south to English Channel.

Goldeneye

Bucephala clangula 40–48 cm (16–19 ins)

Identification Very compact duck with large, domed head
and yellow eyes. Male black and white, with oval white patch
between eye (yellow) and bill, and green-gloss on head. Female
mainly grey with brown head and yellow-tipped bill. Juvenile
male similar to female, but with darker head, hint of white head
patch and all-black bill. Flight level, with rapid wing-beats.
Voice Male has nasal 'wee-wee' in courtship display.
Habitat Breeds on lakes and fast-flowing rivers in the
coniferous forest zone. Outside breeding
season mainly coastal; also on lakes,
reservoirs and larger rivers, especially
at coast.
Breeding range Mainly Scandinavia
and north-eastern Europe. In Britain
and Ireland increasing (about a
hundred pairs, mainly in Scotland).
Movements Winter visitor to Britain
and Ireland (about 15,000 birds), central
and south-eastern Europe.

Common Scoter
Melanitta nigra 46–50 cm (18–20 ins)

Identification Squat, short-necked sea-duck. Male is uniform black; bill black, with orange-yellow spot at base. Female dark brown with pale head and sides of neck. Flight rapid, in irregular strings.

Voice Male has short, fluting 'pyer' courtship call; female 'how-how-how' or 'knarr'.

Habitat Breeds on lakes, mainly in tundra zone. Outside breeding season, mainly at sea, often far from coast.

Breeding range Iceland, Scandinavia; also a rare breeder in Scotland and Ireland (about 150 pairs).

Movements Summer visitor in breeding range. Winters to Atlantic and North Sea coasts, south to Gibraltar.

Velvet Scoter★
Melanitta fusca 53–58 cm (21–23 ins)

Identification Larger than Common Scoter, and has white wing patches (may be hidden when swimming). Male black, with white patch below eye. Female dark brown with pale patches at side of head (sometimes absent). Sometimes mixes with Common Scoter or Eider in winter flocks.

Voice In breeding season, female has a nasal 'braa-braa'; male a piping 'kyu'.

Habitat Breeding season on lakes in mountains, especially in northern coniferous forest and tundra zones. Coastal waters outside breeding season.

Breeding range Scandinavia and around Baltic Sea.

Movements Summer visitor in breeding range. Mainly to North Sea and Baltic coasts as passage bird and winter visitor.

Long-tailed Duck*
Clangula hyemalis
40–55 cm (16–22 ins)

Identification Elegant, short-
billed sea-duck, with striking
brown and white plumage.
Plumage variable through
season, but male nearly always has
long tail streamers. In winter,
plumage mainly white with brown
patch on head, dark brown breast and wings. In breeding
plumage, male has brown upper parts and white area
around eye.
Voice Vocal. Male has melodious goose-like call, audible from
a distance; females 'ark-ark-ark'.
Habitat Breeds on small lakes and slow rivers in Scandinavian
tundra, and at coast. In winter, usually well out to sea.
Breeding range Iceland, Scandinavia, eastern Baltic.
Movements Common winter visitor to southern North Sea,
Baltic and coasts around northern Britain and Ireland.

Smew*
Mergus albellus 36–43 cm (14–17 ins)

Identification Smallest of the sawbill ducks. Steep forehead
and relatively short bill. Male pure white, with black lines on
body, black eye-patch and black back. Female grey, with red-
brown cap, and white cheeks. Eclipse male like female, but with
larger amounts of white on wings. Immature male has brownish
white wing patches. Sometimes seen with Goldeneye in winter.
Dives frequently, and flies fast.
Voice Fairly silent. Male has rasping 'kairrr' as alarm call, or in
courtship; female a quacking 'ga-ga-ga'.
Habitat Breeds at woodland edges and lakes in
northern Europe. Coastal in winter. Also at
inland lakes and reservoirs.
Breeding range Northern and
eastern Scandinavia.
Movements Summer visitor in
breeding range. Winters south
to coasts of North Sea, Baltic and
English Channel.

Goosander

Mergus merganser 57–69 cm (22–27 ins)

Identification Largest European sawbill, with long, hook-tipped red bill. Male mostly white, with salmon-pink flush underneath, greenish black head and black back. Female mainly grey, with brown head and upper neck and white chin and neck.

Voice Normally silent. Breeding male has various high-pitched calls; breeding female a harsh 'skrrark'.

Habitat Breeds on fish-rich lakes and rivers in forested areas, right up into the tundra. In winter, on large lakes and rivers and at coast.

Breeding range Iceland, Scandinavia, around Baltic Sea, north-western Britain (about 2,500 pairs). Also a rare breeder in alpine areas.

Movements Resident and partial migrant in Britain; summer visitor to breeding areas in northern Europe. Winters south to Baltic coasts and inland waters.

Red-breasted Merganser

Mergus serrator 50–60 cm (20–24 ins)

Identification Slightly smaller than Goosander, with similar long, narrow bill. Both sexes have ragged double crest. Female has indistinct boundary between head and neck colouration.

Voice Normally silent. Breeding male has nasal 'qui-qui-air'; female a grating 'aark-aark-aark'.

Habitat Breeds on clear lakes and rivers of northern Europe, and on shallow sandy or stony coasts. Outside breeding season mainly at coasts.

Breeding range Mainly Iceland, Scandinavia and north-western Britain and Ireland.

Total British and Irish population about 3,000 pairs.

Movements Resident and partial migrant in Britain, summer visitor to breeding areas in northern Europe. Winters south to most coasts.

Egyptian Vulture★
Neophron percnopterus 58–66 cm (23–26 ins)

Identification Our smallest vulture, and the palest in adult plumage. In flight, shows small head, long, narrow wings and wedge-shaped tail. Adult creamy white, with black flight feathers. Juvenile dark brown, getting gradually whiter over four years. Sometimes in small groups at carcass, but not very sociable. Glides and soars. Visits rubbish tips, often with Black Kites.

Voice Seldom heard, occasional grunts.
Habitat Mountains, dry rocky country.
Breeding range Mediterranean region.
Movements Summer visitor, but may overwinter in south.

Griffon Vulture★
Gyps fulvus 96–104 cm (38–41 ins)

Identification Most common of the large vultures. Usually seen soaring in flocks on thermal up-draughts, on the look-out for food. Huge, with long, broad wings. Buff-coloured, with dark brown flight feathers. Tail short and rather square.
Voice Croaks and whistles at breeding site.
Habitat Mountains, dry rocky country with cliffs.

Breeding range Mainly south-western and south-eastern Europe (notably Spain and Greece).
Movements Resident and partial migrant.
Similar species Two other large vultures breed in southern Europe, but both species are rare. The BLACK (CINEREOUS) VULTURE★, *Aegypius monachus*, is like a darker version of the Griffon. There are just a few hundred pairs in Europe (Spain, Mallorca and Greece). The LAMMERGEIER★, *Gypaetus barbatus*, is shaped like a huge falcon, with rather pointed wings and long tail (Pyrenees, Corsica, Greece).

Golden Eagle

Aquila chrysaetos 76–90 cm (30–35 ins)

Identification Large, dark, and powerful, with heavy bill and strong talons. Crown and neck golden brown, wings long and relatively narrow. Tail rather long and broad. Juveniles dark with large white patches on wings; tail white with broad black tip.
Voice Occasional yelps, but rarely heard.
Habitat Mainly restricted to remote mountain areas.
Breeding range Scandinavia, Scotland (about 420 pairs), Iberia; also in Alps and Carpathians.
Movements Mainly resident. Young birds wander long distances.

White-tailed Eagle

Haliaeetus albicilla 80–95 cm (31–37 ins)

Identification Huge, with very broad, parallel-sided wings, head well extended, tail short and wedge-shaped. Powerful yellow bill and short white tail. Juveniles (one to four years) dark, even on head, tail and bill.
Voice Very vocal, with a loud raucous 'kyow-kyow-kyow', especially near nest.
Habitat Rocky coasts; also near large forested lakes and rivers, even a few kilometres from water.
Breeding range Norway, northern Germany and Poland. Re-introduction in west of Scotland (about ten pairs).
Movements Resident and partial migrant. Regular on certain large lakes (e.g. in foothills of the Alps) outside breeding season.

Osprey
Pandion haliaetus 50–58 cm (20–23 ins)

Identification Very pale beneath in flight, with long, narrow, angled wings. Dark brown above, mostly white underneath, with brown breast-band. Hovers and plunges to catch fish in talons. Dives almost vertically with wings half closed, often submerges for a short time.
Voice Whistling calls, usually heard near nest.
Habitat Lakes, slow-flowing rivers and coasts. Regular at lakes, reservoirs and rivers on migration.
Breeding range Stable, but small, population in Scotland (about seventy pairs); frequent in Sweden and Finland.
Movements Summer visitor.

Short-toed Eagle★
Circaetus gallicus 63–68 cm (25–27 ins)

Identification Large, with broad head and yellow eye. Underside white, with lines of dark spots. In flight, pale underside contrasts with dark upper chest. Tail is long, narrow and square-ended. Wings sharply angled and held forward when gliding. Soars, glides and hovers when searching for reptile prey.
Voice Quite vocal, especially in breeding season. Whistles and weak barking.
Habitat Open, varied, often dry and rocky landscapes with rich reptile fauna; also found on marshy plains interspersed with heath and woodland.
Breeding range Mainly Spain, France, Greece, Italy. Absent from northern Europe.
Movements Summer visitor.

Buzzard

Buteo buteo 45–53 cm (18–21 ins)

Identification Medium-sized bird of prey
with short neck and large, rounded head.
Wings are broad, and the tail is rounded
when spread. Very variable in plumage, from
almost white to uniform dark brown, but
usually brownish, with paler breast-band.
Eye dark brown to yellow. Rather compact
in flight with wings held somewhat stiffly,
and wing-tips noticeably upturned when
soaring. Occasionally hovers.
Voice Mewing 'heeyair', especially in spring.
Habitat Wooded regions with fields, marshes and hedges.
Hunts over open country, nesting mostly at woodland edges.
Breeding range Most of Europe, except far north. Absent
from most of Ireland (except north), and much of southern
and eastern England (but gradually spreading eastwards).
Movements Resident and partial migrant. Summer visitor to
north-eastern Europe.

Rough-legged Buzzard★

Buteo lagopus 53–63 cm (21–25 ins)

Identification Tail white, with wide dark band at tip; hovers
much more frequently than Buzzard. Plumage variable, but
usually has pale head, and more contrast than Buzzard. Legs
feathered to toes. Wings and tail relatively long, belly black,
contrasting with pale undersides of the wings.
Voice Cat-like mewing. Usually silent in winter.
Habitat Mountains and tundra of northern Europe,
mostly above or beyond tree-line. Numbers increase
after rodent population explosions. In winter,
found mainly on moorland and heaths.
Breeding range Scandinavia
and Finland.
Movements In some winters,
it migrates south in large
numbers, especially to eastern
Europe, but also (in small numbers)
to east coast of Britain.

Red Kite
Milvus milvus 58–64 cm (23–25 ins)

Identification Long wings
and long, deeply forked tail.
Light grey head, pale
patches towards ends of
wings, and red-brown
body. Soars with slightly raised
wings; sometimes hovers with deep,
relatively slow wing-beats; often twists tail in flight.
Voice Whistling cries, often heard in spring;
also single 'deeair' or 'yeee' calls.
Habitat Hilly, wooded landscape, with open areas such as
small wetlands and clearings.
Breeding range Widespread, but scattered in central,
southern and eastern Europe, with outliers in southern
Scandinavia and in Wales (about seventy-five pairs).
Currently being re-introduced to Scotland and England.
Movements Resident in Wales and southern Europe.
Summer visitor and partial migrant in central Europe.

Black Kite★
Milvus migrans 53–60 cm (21–24 ins)

Identification Darker than Red Kite. Long, relatively broad
wings, and long square (sometimes slightly forked) tail. Elegant
in flight, circling with horizontal
wings. Often flies slowly over
water and along river banks in
search of dead fish. Very sociable
outside breeding season.
Voice Gull-like calls and whinnying.
Habitat Breeds near rivers and
lakes; in river valley forests, at
woodland margins, also on cliffs.
Breeding range Southern, central and
eastern Europe. Widespread, but patchy distribution.
Movements Summer visitor. Rare visitor to British Isles.
Similar species The small, kestrel-sized BLACK-WINGED
KITE★, *Elanus caeruleus*, though not strictly similar, is related.
It is rare, but increasing; found mainly in Spain and Portugal.
It is pale grey with black wing patches.

Goshawk
Accipiter gentilis 48–63 cm (18–25 ins)

Identification Large size (especially the female which is Buzzard-sized); long tail and relatively short and rounded wings. Male smaller and lighter than female. Upperparts of male grey-brown to slate grey, female brown. Underside pale, with horizontal speckles; in juveniles yellowish, with dark brown spots.
Voice In breeding season 'gik-gik-gik'; Buzzard-like 'hiair', accented on the first syllable.
Habitat Wooded country, particularly coniferous forests.
Breeding range Widespread, but secretive in most of Europe. In Britain, rare (about 200 pairs).
Movements Resident.

Sparrowhawk
Accipiter nisus 28–40 cm (11–16 ins)

Identification Male smaller than female. Wings rounded, tail long, narrow and square-ended. Underparts narrowly banded, rust-brown in male. Female brownish grey above, male blue-grey. Juveniles dark brown above, barred below.
Voice Alarm call (usually near nest) a high-pitched 'kyi-kyi-kyi'.
Habitat Mainly wooded country, but increasingly suburban.
Breeding range Widespread in most of Europe. In British Isles, common and increasing (about 45,000 pairs).
Movements Resident. Summer visitor in far north.

Honey Buzzard
Pernis apivorus
50–59 cm (20–23 ins)

Identification Buzzard-sized, but slimmer and with longer wings and tail. Plumage variable: upperside usually dark brown, underside pale, almost white, or uniform brown. Head grey, eye yellow. In flight, shows outstretched head, relatively narrow wings and long, narrow tail with one or two clear dark bands and black tip.

Voice On breeding ground, a high-pitched, melodious 'kee-er'.

Habitat Mixed woodland with clearings, pasture and fields. Usually nests at woodland edge, hunting in open areas.

Breeding range Most of Europe, except far north and west. Rare bird (at edge of range) in Britain (about twenty pairs).

Movements Summer visitor.

Marsh Harrier
Circus aeruginosus 48–55 cm (19–22 ins)

Identification Buzzard-sized, but slimmer and narrower-winged and with longer tail. Male has pale grey tail and upper wings, contrasting with otherwise dark plumage and black wing-tips. Female dark, with cream coloured head and shoulders. Flight slow, interspersed with buoyant gliding, wings held in a V-shape.

Voice Male has squawking 'quiair'; alarm call a snarling 'kike-kike-kike'.

Habitat Marshes and lakes with extensive reed beds. Hunts over reeds, water meadows, fields and open country.

Breeding range Much of Europe, except extreme north and west. In British Isles, mainly in south and east (about a hundred pairs).

Movements Resident in south and west of range, summer visitor in the east.

Hen Harrier
Circus cyaneus 48–55 cm (19–22 ins)

Identification Slim and light in flight. Male has ash-grey plumage, with contrasting black-tipped wings and white rump. Female is dark brown above, pale yellow-brown beneath, with striped wings and tail, and clear white rump. Flight buoyant and gliding.
Voice Male has a high-pitched 'piuu piuu' in courtship flight; female a hoarse 'pih-e'. Alarm call 'chek-ek-ek-ek'.
Habitat Open landscapes: heather moor, dunes, marshes and damp meadows; also in young plantations. In winter, regular in open marshland and wet heath.
Breeding range Much of central and northern Europe. In British Isles, mainly in north and west (about 800 pairs).
Movements Resident and partial migrant in western and central Europe. Summer visitor in northern Europe.

Montagu's Harrier
Circus pygargus 40–46 cm (16–18 ins)

Identification Very slim and graceful in flight (recalls seagull, or even tern). Male similar to Hen Harrier, but with narrower wings and longer tail, black band on wings and brown stripes on belly. Female almost identical to female Hen Harrier, but wings narrower and white rump less marked. Juveniles like female, but with red-brown undersides.
Voice Shrill 'ke-kek-kek'.
Habitat Breeds in low vegetation near water, but also in damp heath, especially on fens, and increasingly in open fields. Hunts mainly over wetlands with low cover, and in cultivated fields.
Breeding range Much of central and southern Europe. Rare breeder in British Isles (about ten pairs).
Movements Summer visitor.

Peregrine
Falco peregrinus
40–54 cm (16–21 ins)

Identification Crow-sized,
powerful falcon. Pointed broad-
based wings; short, tapering tail.
Broad, dark moustache. Underparts
pale, with dark barring. Juveniles
dark brown above, yellow-brown
beneath, with heavy, dark streaks.
Normal flight relatively slow, with powerful, shallow wing-
beats, and periods of gliding.
Voice 'Kek-kek-kek' at nest-site.
Habitat Hilly and mountainous areas, and at coast. Needs
steep rocks or cliffs for nest-site. Estuaries and other wetlands
in winter.
Breeding range Most of Europe, notably British Isles,
France and Spain. In British Isles, about 1,500 pairs, mainly
in north and west.
Movements Resident, except in far north, where summer
visitor.

Hobby
Falco subbuteo 33–38 cm (13–15 ins)

Identification Flight outline like a large swift. Kestrel-sized,
but with shorter tail and long, sickle-shaped wings. Upperparts
blue-grey, head with conspicuous moustache. Leg feathers and
under tail coverts rusty red.
Voice 'Kew-kew-kew', and 'ki-ki-ki-ki'.
Habitat Wooded country with heath land, damp
meadows and lakes or gravel pits. Breeds in light
woodland, at forest edges and in lone trees in
fields.
Breeding range Most of Europe, except
north and west. In British Isles, mainly in
southern and eastern England, where
increased in recent years (from about sixty
pairs in the 1950s to over 1,000 pairs in
the 1990s).
Movements Summer visitor.

Kestrel

Falco tinnunculus 33–39 cm (13–15 ins)

Identification Most common small bird of
prey, often seen by main roads; hovers
frequently. Small falcon with long tail,
long, pointed wings and brown
upperparts. Male has weakly speckled,
red-brown back, grey head
and grey tail with broad terminal
band. Female uniformly red-brown,
with barred upperparts.
Voice High-pitched, rapid 'kikikiki'.
Habitat Open countryside, breeding in trees in fields and
at woodland edges; also in rocky country and in villages
and cities.
Breeding range Most of Europe. In British Isles, about
60,000 pairs.
Movements Resident. Summer visitor in northern and
eastern Europe.
Similar species LESSER KESTREL*, *Falco naumanni*, is
slightly smaller. It is a rather rare species of southern Europe
(especially Spain and Turkey).

Merlin

Falco columbarius
26–31 cm (10–12 ins)

Identification Smallest of our falcons,
with low, rapid flight. Male is grey above,
rusty yellow underneath with long dark
streaks. Female has larger streaks below
and is dark brown above, with a barred
tail. Juveniles very like female.
Voice Very rapid 'kikiki', usually
near nest.
Habitat Upland birch woodland,
heather moors, dunes. In winter, often
at coast or wash land.
Breeding range Northern and north-western Europe.
In British Isles, recent decline to about 600 pairs.
Movements Resident in north-western Europe, summer
visitor in Scandinavia.

Willow★ and Red Grouse

Lagopus lagopus 40–43 cm (16–17 ins)

Identification The Red Grouse is the British and Irish subspecies of the Willow Grouse. Both sexes are reddish brown, with black barring. The Willow Grouse (shown here) has white wings, and turns pure white in winter (see Ptarmigan). Flies strongly and glides on drooping wings.

Voice 'Go-back, go-back, go-back'.

Habitat Upland heather-moor and bog. Willow Grouse also found in scrub.

Breeding range Scandinavia (Willow Grouse) and British Isles (Red Grouse). In British Isles, most common in northern England and Scotland.

Movements Resident.

Ptarmigan

Lagopus mutus 33–36 cm (13–14 ins)

Identification Slightly smaller than Red/Willow Grouse. Wings are white at all seasons (like Willow Grouse). Breeding male marbled dark brown-grey on upperside and breast, otherwise white, with small, red comb. Female yellow-brown, with darker crescent-shaped markings. In winter, pure white, except for jet-black tail, male with black stripe through eye.

Voice Characteristic grating call of male 'arrr-arr-krrr-ak-ak-ak'.

Habitat Above tree-line in rocky sites. At lower levels in winter.

Breeding range Iceland, Scandinavia, Scotland, Alps.

Movements Resident.

Black Grouse
Tetrao tetrix
Male: 51–56 cm (20–22 ins);
female 40–44 cm (16–17 ins)

Identification Male has shiny, blue-
black plumage and lyre-shaped tail
feathers, fluffed out during courtship to
reveal white under tail coverts. Female is smaller, with
camouflaged grey-brown plumage. Bill slightly hooked. Rapid
wing-beats interspersed with periods of gliding. Often perches
in trees.
Voice Male song at display ground is a bubbling coo,
interspersed with hissing or sneezing.
Habitat Heather moor and bog, open wooded areas; dwarf
shrub heath near tree-line.
Breeding range Britain, Scandinavia and north-eastern
Europe, south to Alps. Absent from Ireland. About 10,000
breeding females (steady decline).
Movements Resident.

Capercaillie
Tetrao urogallus
Male 82–90 cm (32–35 ins); female 58–64 cm (23–25 ins)

Identification Largest grouse. Male turkey-sized, black, with
long spreadable tail. Female smaller, with orange-brown breast-
band and rusty-red, black-banded tail. Take-off noisy, flight
rapid with powerful wing-beats and long glides.
Voice Courting male has strange
explosive, grinding and gurgling
calls.
Habitat Coniferous and mixed
forests, with small clearings.
Breeding range Scandinavia,
Scotland (about 1,500 birds),
central and south-eastern Europe.
Decline due to destruction of
natural Scots Pine forests, and
through disturbance.
Movements Resident.

Hazelhen (Hazel Grouse)★

Bonasa bonasia 35–37 cm (14–15 ins)

Identification Small and secretive grouse. Grey above, spotted buff below. Male has black bib and slight crest. Both sexes have black band on tail.
Voice Thin, high-pitched whistle.
Habitat Coniferous (especially spruce) forest, with birch and alder.
Breeding range Central, northern and eastern Europe, west to eastern France and southern Norway.
Movements Resident.

Pheasant

Phasianus colchicus
Male 75–88 cm (30–35 ins); female 53–63 cm (21–25 ins)

Identification Male has striking bronze plumage, red face wattle, shiny green neck (sometimes with white ring) and very long, pointed tail. Female yellow-brown with dark speckles and somewhat shorter tail.
Voice Male has explosive 'gergock', often followed by wing-flapping.
Habitat Found mainly in cultivated areas and at edges of light woodland. Also in reed beds and fen carr.
Breeding range Native of southern Asia; introduced to Europe for sport. Much of Europe, except far north and far south.
Movements Resident.

Red-legged Partridge
Alectoris rufa 33–36 cm (13–14 ins)

Identification Rounded shape, barred flanks and distinctive white face mask with black border. Flies low, with wings bowed.
Voice 'Chuk-chuk-er', also grating 'shreck-shreck'.
Habitat Prefers dry, stony fields, sandy heaths and chalk downland.
Breeding range France, northern Italy, Spain and Portugal. Introduced to Britain where most common in south and east. Rare in Ireland.
Movements Resident.

Grey Partridge
Perdix perdix 29–32 cm (11–13 ins)

Identification Small and dumpy, with short tail. Rusty brown stripes on flank, and dark, horseshoe-shaped patch on breast. Flight rapid. Glides with wings bowed.
Voice Alarm call a loud 'kerripriprip'. Territorial males a hoarse, repeated 'girreck', mainly in morning and evening.
Habitat Lowland cultivated country, with agricultural fields, pasture, hedges and overgrown field margins; also heaths.
Breeding range Much of Europe, except far north and far south. In Britain, rather rare in extreme west. Rare in Ireland. Declining due to more intensive cultivation and decrease in food and cover.
Movements Resident.

Quail

Coturnix coturnix 17–18 cm (6–7 ins)

Identification Smallest member of European partridge family. Dumpy, almost tail-less, with camouflaged plumage. Male has black markings on head and chin; female has heavily speckled chest. Secretive, more often heard than seen.
Voice Male territorial call is a repeated 'wick-wick-ic' (accented on first syllable), heard by day or night.
Habitat Mixed fields with rough margins, hedges. Breeds in winter wheat, clover and lucerne crops, and in hay-meadows.
Breeding range Mainly southern and central Europe, north to British Isles. Widespread in lowlands, but generally decreasing. Normally rather rare in British Isles (about 300 pairs), but population fluctuates.
Movements Summer visitor. Resident in Mediterranean.

Corncrake

Crex crex 25–28 cm (10–11 ins)

Identification Slim, long-legged. Upperparts light grey-brown, with dark brown streaks on back. Flight ungainly and fluttering with trailing legs and showing chestnut wings. Rarely seen, as usually remains hidden in vegetation.
Voice Male has rasping 'rerrp-rerrp', often continuing for hours, by night as well as in the daytime.
Habitat Damp grassland, traditionally cropped hay meadows; also in crops such as cereals, lucerne and clover.
Breeding range Mainly central and eastern Europe. In British Isles, highly endangered and declining (about 450 pairs); mainly in Ireland and Hebrides. Populations in decline following habitat destruction and mechanized hay-gathering.
Movements Summer visitor.

Coot
Fulica atra
36–40 cm (14–16 ins)

Identification Black,
rather dumpy water bird
with grey-green legs and
white frontal shield above
white bill. Toes lobed at edges. Dives for submerged food.
Often gathers in large flocks in winter.
Voice Male an unmusical 'tsk', and a sound like a cork
popping. Female has a loud, barking 'kurff'. Alarm call is a
sharp 'psi'.
Habitat Lakes, reservoirs, ponds, and slow-flowing rivers with
well developed fringing vegetation; also on gravel pits and on
lakes in urban parks.
Breeding range Most of Europe except far north. In British
Isles, common except in north-western Scotland.
Movements Resident and partial migrant. Summer visitor
to north-eastern Europe.

Moorhen
Gallinula chloropus 31–35 cm (12–14 ins)

Identification Smaller and slimmer than Coot, with red,
yellow-tipped bill and red frontal shield. Legs and long toes
green. White under tail coverts displayed as tail bobbed.
Juveniles grey-brown with pale chin. Trails legs in flight. Nods
head while swimming and walking, and repeatedly bobs tail.
Voice Alarm call a guttural 'krrrk', or penetrating 'kirreck'.
Habitat Still and slow-flowing water, ditches and small,
overgrown ponds; also common on streams and in ponds in
urban parks and gardens.
Feeds mainly on land.
Breeding range Most of
Europe except far north
and north-east. In British
Isles, common except in
north-western Scotland.
Movements Resident.
Summer visitor to north-
eastern Europe.

Water Rail
Rallus aquaticus 27–29 cm (10–11 ins)

Identification Slim marsh bird with long, slightly decurved red bill, and black and white striped flanks. Upperparts brown with black markings; face, neck and breast slate grey; under tail coverts white. Juveniles are pale brown below, with delicate stripes on neck and breast, and less stripy flanks. Secretive and difficult to observe.
Voice Like pigs squealing: 'kriek-krruie-krruie'; in spring, a sharp 'zik-zik-zik' call, often ending with an extended, throaty 'tjuier'.
Habitat Thick reed and sedge beds, especially at river or lake margins. Sometimes along ditches.
Breeding range Most of Europe, except far north-east. Resident in British Isles, most common in Ireland and parts of East Anglia. Total British Isles population probably around 3,000 pairs.
Movements Resident. Summer visitor in eastern Europe.

Baillon's Crake★
Porzana pusilla 17–18 cm (6.5–7 ins)

Identification Smallest crake. Male has more contrasting plumage than Little Crake, with more marked barring on flanks, and uniformly green bill. Very rarely seen.
Voice Rattling frog-like trill 'trrr-trrr-trrr'.
Habitat River deltas, fens, swamps, ponds with dense cover.
Breeding range Mainly western and southern Europe, notably Spain.
Movements Summer visitor. Rare vagrant to Britain.

Little Crake★

Porzana parva
18–20 cm (7–8 ins)

Identification Smaller than
Spotted Crake. Bill is
yellow-green with red at base.
Upperparts olive brown with lighter
and darker longitudinal stripes and rows of indistinct white
spots. Underside slate grey. Under tail coverts clearly barred,
flanks weakly barred. Female cream-coloured below and with
whitish chin. Rarely seen.
Voice In spring, the female has a rapid, descending trill: 'pep-
perrr'. Alarm call of both sexes a sharp 'tvook'. Male's song,
usually heard at dusk, is an accelerating 'put-put-put-purrr'.
Habitat Thick reed and sedge beds in shallow water.
Breeding range Scattered, mainly in central and eastern
Europe, but also eastern Spain.
Movements Summer visitor. Rare vagrant to Britain.

Spotted Crake

Porzana porzana 22–24 cm (8–9 ins)

Identification Tiny marsh bird, scarcely as big as
Blackbird, with dark, speckled plumage.
Flanks barred white; under tail
coverts yellowish. Bill much
shorter than Water Rail's.
Juveniles have whiter chin and
paler undersides. Very rarely seen;
lives in thick vegetation.
Voice Male's spring song is
characteristic: a short, repeated,
'huitt', like a whiplash, usually at dusk
and at night. Other sounds include 'keck' or growling 'brurr'.
Habitat Fenland, edges of rivers and lakes, particularly where
reeds give way to sedges; also in wet meadows and ditch
margins.
Breeding range Most of Europe, except far north and south.
Rare and decreasing, absent over large areas. In British Isles, a
rare breeder (about twenty pairs).
Movements Resident in south of range, summer visitor
further north (including British Isles).

Crane

Grus grus 106–118 cm (42–46 ins)

Identification Tall, elegant and long-legged with long bill (but relatively shorter than heron or egret). Mainly grey, with black and white on head and neck. In flight, neck is extended and legs trail well beyond tail. Migrating flocks often fly in wedge formation.

Voice Loud bellowing or trumpeting call 'krooi-kruh', often in early morning.

Habitat Extensive wetlands, marshy lake margins, swampy woodland, bogs and isolated forest lakes. On migration also found in cultivated areas, roosting on shallow water.

Breeding range Mainly Scandinavia, northern Germany, Poland and Baltic States. Irregular breeder in Britain (one to two pairs).

Movements Summer visitor.

Stone Curlew

Burhinus oedicnemus 38–43 cm (15–17 ins)

Identification Large wader with short bill, large yellow eyes and long, relatively thick, yellow legs. In flight, shows double white wing-bars and black and white primaries.

Voice Curlew-like, fluting 'keer-lee'; often as duet at dusk; flight-call 'gigigigigi'.

Habitat Steppe areas, heath land. Dry, open areas with sparse plant cover and sandy or stony soil and low vegetation. Occasionally at coast during migration.

Breeding range Patchy distribution in western, central and southern Europe (mainly Spain, Portugal and France). Absent from northern Europe (including Ireland). Rare breeder in Britain (about 150 pairs).

Movements Resident in southern Mediterranean, summer visitor elsewhere.

Great Bustard★

Otis tarda
Male 95–105 cm (37–41 ins); female 75–85 cm (30–33 ins)

Identification Large, turkey-
like male larger than female.
Head and neck grey; wings, back
and tail chestnut, speckled black.
Legs long and thick. Wings
white, with black trailing edge.
Voice Barks and squeals in
breeding season.
Habitat Open plains, grassy
steppes, crops.
Breeding range Scattered in Iberia,
central and eastern Europe (especially
Hungary).
Movements Resident.

Little Bustard★

Tetrax tetrax 40–45 cm (16–18 ins)

Identification Smaller than Great Bustard. Grey-brown
above, white below. Male has grey chin, and black and white
markings on neck. Wings show large expanse of white in flight.
Forms large flocks in winter.
Voice Snorting calls in
breeding season. Wings produce
whistling noise in flight.
Habitat Steppes, cornfields and
other crops.
Breeding range Mainly Spain,
Portugal, France, Italy.
Movements Resident and partial
migrant. Summer visitor in north of
range.

Ringed Plover
Charadrius hiaticula 18–20 cm (7–8 ins)

Identification Small wader with sandy brown upperparts, black and white face pattern and orange-yellow legs. In flight, shows clear white wing-bar. Bill orange, tipped with black. Outside breeding plumage, bill is black with orange mark at base. Juveniles resemble winter adults, but upperside feathers look scaly. Runs rapidly over sand, often stopping abruptly.

Voice Alarm call a soft 'tee-ip' or 'dooi', and a rapid 'kip-kiwip'. Song is a rapid 'drui-drui-drui' given in flight.

Habitat Coastal sand and shingle, and on salt lakes. On migration, regular on inland sand or mud banks.

Breeding range Coasts of northern and western Europe. In British Isles, common on coasts, especially in north and east.

Movements Resident and partial migrant. Summer visitor in north of range; visits coasts of south-western Europe in winter.

Little Ringed Plover
Charadrius dubius 14–16 cm (5–6 ins)

Identification Small, rotund wader with black and white face pattern (in breeding season), muddy yellow legs and yellow eye-ring. Smaller than Ringed Plover and lacking white wing-bar.

Voice Alarm call a loud melancholy 'piu' or sharp 'pitt-pitt'. Breeding song a trilling 'tree-tree-tree'.

Habitat Gravelly and sandy river banks and islands, gravel and sand pits, fish ponds and flooded quarries. On migration, mainly at coast, or river mud.

Breeding range Much of Europe except far north and west. Very rare in Ireland. In Britain, mainly in Midlands and southern England (about 1,000 pairs).

Movements Summer visitor.

Kentish Plover★
Charadrius alexandrinus 15–17 cm (6–7 ins)

Identification Longer-legged than other ringed plovers, and with less black on face. Breeding male has chestnut on head. Bill and feet are dark, and neck band is incomplete. Female and winter male have paler plumage. In flight, shows white wing-bar.
Voice Alarm call 'brrr-brrr'; flight-call 'pit'. Song a trill, often in flight.
Habitat Most coastal of plovers, usually seen near to tidal zone on sandy coasts; also on lagoons and saltpans.
Breeding range Spain, Portugal, France. Mainly in Mediterranean, Atlantic and (more rarely) southern North Sea; also breeds inland in Hungary and eastern Austria, and further east around Black Sea.
Movements Resident and partial migrant. Rare visitor to British Isles on migration.

Turnstone★
Arenaria interpres 21–24 cm (8–9 in)

Identification Short-legged and dumpy wader. Breeding plumage very colourful chequered pattern. In winter, duller brownish black with pale feather edges. In flight, shows broad white wing-bar and white tail with black band near tip.
Voice Flight-call a rapid 'tri-tri-tri' or 'tuk-a-tuk'. Song a nasal 'tivi-tivi-tititi', from song-post or in flight.
Habitat Breeds on rocky coasts, islands and in moss and lichen tundra of northern Europe. Winters on stony or pebbly coasts.
Breeding range Coasts of Scandinavia and northern Baltic.
Movements Summer visitor to breeding grounds. Winters mainly to coasts of North Sea and Atlantic.

Lapwing
Vanellus vanellus
28–31 cm (11–12 ins)

Identification Black and white
plumage, with long, curved crest
on head. Female has shorter crest
and paler chin. Outside breeding
season, upperside paler and crest shorter. Tumbling courtship
flight in spring. Forms large flocks in the autumn and winter
(sometimes with Black-headed Gulls and Golden Plovers).
Voice Whiny, hoarse 'peewee' or 'kee-vit'; courtship flight
produces humming noises from wings.
Habitat Breeds in damp meadows, bogs, coastal pasture, wet
heath, fields and farmland.
Breeding range Most of Europe, becoming scarcer towards
the south. The most common breeding wader in British Isles
(about 250,000 pairs).
Movements Resident and partial migrant in British Isles.
Summer visitor in north of range.

Dotterel
Charadrius morinellus
20–22 cm (8–9 ins)

Identification Prominent white
stripe above eye, meeting behind
head to form V-shape. Female
slightly larger and more colourful than
male. Black belly in breeding plumage. In winter, much paler
with yellow-grey upperparts, white belly and less clear breast-
band and eye-stripe. Dumpy and short-tailed in flight, with no
wing-bar. Often very approachable.
Voice Flight-call 'kirr' or 'plitt'. Song a repeated 'pit-pit-pit',
in display flight.
Habitat Breeds on open tundra. Outside breeding season,
seen in small groups on dry, rocky areas, short pasture and
riverbanks.
Breeding range Northern Scandinavia, northern Britain
(mainly Scottish Highlands); also in a few places in the Alps,
Apennines and, more recently, on the Netherlands coast.
British population about 900 pairs.
Movements Summer visitor. Regularly seen on passage at
traditional sites.

Golden Plover
Pluvialis apricaria 26–29 cm (10–11 ins)

Identification In breeding plumage, speckled gold above, jet-black neck and belly with white curving dividing line from face to tail. Amount of black on underside is variable and sometimes lacking completely. In winter, plumage much duller, without black. Winter flocks on fields can look very thrush-like, both in colouration and behaviour.

Voice Soft 'dui'. Alarm call a sharp 'tlie', also a plaintive, musical 'tlooi-fee'. Song consists of high trilling whistles.

Habitat Breeds on damp mountain tundra in northern Europe and on moorland in coniferous forest zone; in central Europe on raised bogs. Common in meadows, pasture and fields in winter, often in large flocks.

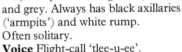

Breeding range Mainly Iceland, Scandinavia and northern Britain (mainly Scotland and northern Pennines). British population about 23,000 pairs;Ireland about 400 pairs.

Movements Resident and partial migrant. Numbers swelled by migrants from further north in winter.

Grey Plover★
Pluvialis squatarola 27–30 cm (11–12 ins)

Identification Slightly larger than Golden Plover, and with heavier bill. Greyer than Golden Plover in winter plumage. Breeding plumage (rarely seen) richly contrasting black, white and grey. Always has black axillaries ('armpits') and white rump. Often solitary.

Voice Flight-call 'tlee-u-ee'.

Habitat Breeds in Arctic lichen tundra. In winter, mainly on mud flats or sandy shores.

Breeding range High Arctic of northern Russia.

Movements Regular migrant and winter visitor to most coasts.

Snipe
Gallinago gallinago
25–27 cm (10–11 ins)

Identification Medium-sized wader
with very long bill and camouflaged
plumage. Back brown with black and
yellow markings. Dark stripes on cap.
When flushed, can fly up suddenly,
then pitch to side, calling.
Voice Repeated nasal 'etch' when flushed. Song is a repeated,
'ticka-ticka-ticka', often from a song-post. Male makes high,
undulating flights over breeding ground, plunging down and
producing 'drumming' by vibrating the stiff outer tail feathers.
Habitat Breeds in fens, bogs, damp meadows and other
wetland areas; also seen at mud banks, ponds and ditches.
Breeding range Northern and central Europe. Common in
British Isles, especially in north and west.
Movements Resident and partial migrant. Numbers swelled
by migrants from further north in winter.
Similar species JACK SNIPE*, *Lymnocryptes minimus*, is
smaller and shorter-billed. Regular winter visitor to coasts.

Curlew
Numenius arquata 50–60 cm (20–24 ins)

Identification Largest European wader, with long, decurved
bill. Speckled brown plumage, with white rump and lower
back. Legs long and strong. Flight strong and
gull-like, often in lines or formation.
Voice Flight-call a fluting 'tlooi'.
Spring song is loud fluting calls
accelerating into trill, given by male
during rising and falling song-flight.
Habitat Bogs and upland moors, overgrown lake
margins; also breeds on damp hay meadows and
wet meadows. Mud flats and estuaries outside
breeding season.
Breeding range North and north-eastern Europe.
Common in British Isles (about 50,000 pairs).
Movements Resident in British Isles, mainly summer visitor to
breeding grounds elsewhere. Winters to European coasts,
especially to north-western Europe. In British Isles, numbers
swelled by migrants from further north in winter.

Woodcock
Scolopax rusticola
33–35 cm (13–14 ins)

Identification Short-legged, large-headed wader with long straight bill and highly camouflaged plumage. Flight soft and usually silent, almost owl-like. In display flight ('roding'), male describes low circuits in weak zigzag curves, grunting. Wings broad and rounded, bill held angled towards ground. Crepuscular and nocturnal.
Voice Occasional high-pitched 'tsveet' when disturbed. Roding male alternates deep 'kvorr-kvorr-kvorr' with very high-pitched sharp 'pitsick'.
Habitat Mixed woodland with clearings, rich herb- and shrub-layer, and damp areas.
Breeding range Mainly northern and eastern Europe; patchy further south. British Isles population is around 25,000 pairs.
Movements Winters scattered through Europe, notably in France, British Isles, Spain and Italy.

Whimbrel
Numenius phaeopus 40–46 cm (16–18 ins)

Identification Like a smaller version of Curlew, with somewhat shorter, less smoothly curved bill (bill has rather kinked curve). Upperparts more contrastingly patterned; head with two broad, dark brown stripes. Faster wing-beats than Curlew.
Voice Flight-call a Cuckoo-like 'pu-hu-hu-hu'. Song rather like Curlew's, but trill section harsher.
Habitat Breeds on moorland and wet heath in coniferous forest zone and tundra. On migration at coast, mainly on mud flats, but also on rocky coasts.
Breeding range Iceland, Scandinavia, north-eastern Europe; also extreme north of Scotland (about 465 pairs; increasing).
Movements Summer visitor and passage migrant. Winters mainly on western African coast.

Bar-tailed Godwit*

Limosa lapponica 33–42 cm (13–16 ins)

Identification Medium-sized wader with rather long legs and long, very slightly upturned bill. Breeding male mainly rust-red, speckled brown and black on the back; female and winter male buff-coloured. In flight, legs extend slightly beyond tail, no wing-bar. Tail with narrow bars.
Voice Flight-call 'kirrik-kirrik'. Small flocks often silent.
Habitat Breeds on damp tundra and mires at edge of conifer limit. On migration, mainly on coastal mud flats.
Breeding range Far north of Scandinavia and Russia.
Movements Summer visitor to breeding grounds. Winter visitor and passage migrant to coasts of western Europe. About 80,000 birds visit British Isles each winter (main wintering area, along with Netherlands coast).

Black-tailed Godwit

Limosa limosa 36–44 cm (14–17 ins)

Identification Large, long-legged, long-billed wader. Adult in breeding plumage has rust-brown neck and breast. In winter, both sexes uniform grey. In flight, shows white wing-bar and white base to black tail. Legs longer than those of Bar-tailed Godwit, and bill longer and straight.
Voice Flight-call 'reeka-reeka-reeka'. Song in flight repeated 'keveeyoo-keveeyoo'.
Habitat Breeds mainly in water meadows. In winter, on estuaries and marshes; also on inland shallow water.
Breeding range Iceland, Netherlands, northern Germany, southern Baltic and scattered elsewhere. About fifty pairs breed in Britain, and a handful in Ireland.
Movements Summer visitor and migrant. Winters mainly around coasts.

Redshank

Tringa totanus 27–29 cm (10–11 ins)

Identification Bright red legs, white rump and broad, white, trailing edge to wings (prominent in flight). In breeding plumage, upperparts brownish, with darker speckles; at other times, paler grey-brown above and less speckled. Juveniles lack red base to bill, have yellower legs and are more reddish brown above.

Voice Loud fluting 'tleu-hu' or 'tleu-hu-hu' flight-calls are very characteristic sounds of wetlands and coasts. Alarm call 'tjuk-tjuk-tjuk'. Song a yodelling 'tooli-tooli-tooli', often in flight.

Habitat Breeds in open marshes, mires and salt marshes, especially near coasts. Outside breeding season, on low-lying coasts often in flocks on mud flats or in smaller groups at wet sites inland.

Breeding range Scattered through Europe, but densest in north and east. About 35,000 pairs in British Isles.

Movements Resident and partial migrant. Numbers in British Isles are swelled in autumn and winter by migrants.

Spotted Redshank*

Tringa erythropus
29–32 cm (11–13 ins)

Identification Somewhat larger than Redshank, and with a longer bill and legs. In breeding plumage (rarely seen), mainly blackish, with fine white spots on back; legs dark red. At other times, resembles Redshank, but paler. Lacks wing-bar, but shows white in rump and back.

Voice Flight-call a distinctive sharp 'tchuit'. When disturbed at breeding ground, a penetrating 'tjick-tjick-tjick-tjick'. Song melodious, often in flight.

Habitat Breeds on mires surrounded by forest in far north-east of Europe. Outside breeding season, in small flocks at shallow water and tidal channels on low-lying coasts.

Breeding range North-eastern Scandinavia, Finland and CIS.

Movements Summer visitor to breeding areas. Migrates to Africa and coasts of southern and western Europe.

Greenshank
Tringa nebularia
30–35 cm (12–14 ins)

Identification Large, rather pale grey
wader with long, slightly upturned bill
and long, greenish legs. Outside
breeding season, adults (and juveniles)
paler and greyer above, white beneath.
In flight, the legs extend well beyond tail.
Voice Characteristic flight-call a fluting 'tew-tew-tew'.
On breeding ground, a harder 'kji-kji-kji'. Song a fluting
'klivi-klivi-klivi', often in flight over territory.
Habitat Breeds on open moorland, or on heath with bushes
or isolated trees close to water; also in willow region of northern
mountains and in tundra. Outside breeding season mainly
coastal, in small groups or individually. Also on gravelly or
sandy river margins and flooded meadows.
Breeding range Mainly northern and north-eastern Europe.
Also in north-west of Scotland (about 1,500 pairs).
Movements Summer visitor to breeding grounds. Migrates
to coasts in autumn and winter.

Common Sandpiper
Actitis hypoleucos
19–21 cm (7–8 ins)

Identification Small, short-legged
wader with rather short, straight bill and
dark rump. White wing-bar is clearly
visible in flight. Often bobs tail. Flies
low over water with whirring wing-beats, interspersed with
gliding on down-curved wings.
Voice Shrill 'hee-dee-dee' when flushed. Song, given mostly in
flight, 'heedee-tititi-veedee-titi-veedee', often at night.
Habitat Clear rivers, streams and lakes, and rocky islands with
relatively sparse vegetation. Also on rocky shores with loose
tree stands. Outside breeding season, on gravelly or stony
ponds, lakes and rivers, sewage farms and estuaries.
Breeding range Scattered through most of Europe, becoming
more common towards north and north-east (common in
Finland and Scandinavia). In British Isles, about 18,000 pairs.
Movements Summer visitor and passage migrant.

Green Sandpiper★
Tringa ochropus
21–24 cm (8–9.5 ins)

Identification Medium-sized
wader with dark upperparts and white
base of tail. Tail white, with three to four
brownish bars. Juveniles have yellowish
spots above. Shy, often sitting tight until
flushed (disturbed).

Voice Characteristic flight-call is a sharp 'tluit-tit-tit',
especially when flushed. Alarm call at breeding ground an
incessant 'tick-tick-tick'. Song, given in circling flight, is
fluting 'titti-looee, titti-looee'.

Habitat Breeds on lightly wooded mires, in damp, swampy
woodland and wooded lake margins. On migration rarely on
shore or mud flats. Seen at lakes, often hidden alongside banks.
Also in ditches, marshes, sewage farms and streams.

Breeding range Scandinavia and north-eastern Europe.

Movements Summer visitor to breeding grounds. Migrates to
southern and western Europe in autumn and winter. In British
Isles, small numbers visit regularly as migrants.

Wood Sandpiper
Tringa glareola 19–21 cm (7–8 ins)

Identification Medium-sized
wader, resembling Green Sandpiper, but
more delicate and with slightly longer legs
(visible beyond tail in flight). Also has paler,
more heavily spotted plumage, and paler
head and neck. Heavily spotted with white
above, less clearly marked in winter. Juveniles
with regular yellowish markings on back. Otherwise differs by
pale underwing and less contrasting upperside.

Voice Flight-call 'jiff-jiff-jiff'. Song includes 'tleea-tleea-tleea',
in high song-flight over territory.

Habitat Breeds near water on mires with individual trees, in
swampy woodland and in the tundra. On migration, in small
flocks on open mud, flooded meadows; often at coast.

Breeding range Mainly north-eastern Europe (Finland and
Sweden). Very rare breeder in Scotland (about six pairs).

Movements Migrates to Africa and south Europe in autumn.
Small numbers visit British Isles as passage migrants (autumn).

Little Stint*
Calidris minuta
12–14 cm (5–6 ins)

Identification Tiny wader with short, black bill and black legs. In breeding plumage, has reddish brown upperparts with black and brown spots on the back; white below. V-shaped cream marking on upper back (very clear in juveniles). Dark streak along centre of crown. In winter, grey above, with greyish tinge to breast sides.
Voice Quiet vibrating 'tirr-tirr-tirrit' when flushed. Flight-call 'bit'. Song a soft, tinkling trill, in song-flight.
Habitat Breeds in damp tundra. On migration, mainly at coast (especially muddy estuaries) in small or mixed flocks.
Breeding range Tundra of high Arctic.
Movements Summer visitor to breeding grounds. Migrates to Africa and southern European coasts in autumn. In British Isles, small numbers (mostly juveniles) visit regularly as passage migrants (mainly autumn).

Purple Sandpiper
Calidris maritima
20–22 cm (8–9 ins)

Identification Small dark, dumpy wader with highly camouflaged plumage and with a rather plump, rounded breast. Larger and with shorter legs than Dunlin. Bill about as long as head, dark, with yellow base and slightly decurved. Legs grey-green. When breeding, back is blackish, flecked with rusty brown and pale markings. In winter, mainly dark brownish grey with a pale belly, and pale orange legs. Dark in flight, with narrow white wing-bar, black centre to rump edged white. Relatively tame.
Voice Usually silent in winter. Flight-call 'veet' or 'vitveet'. Song fluting, from ground or in whirring song-flight.
Habitat Breeds on bare, stony plateaux. Otherwise in small flocks on rocky coasts and jetties, often in surf.
Breeding range Mainly Iceland and Scandinavia. Very rare breeder in Scotland (two to three pairs).
Movements Resident and partial migrant. Locally regular in autumn and winter at rocky coasts of north-western Europe.

Temminck's Stint

Calidris temminckii 12–14 cm (5–6 ins)

Identification Similar to Little
Stint, but slightly shorter-
legged. Legs paler, plumage
greyer above.
Voice Flight-call 'tirr'. Tittering
song-flight.
Habitat Breeds on rivers and lake
margins in willow and birch zones
of northern Europe. On migration, on
banks of inland pools and lakes, as well as at coasts.
Breeding range High Arctic and Scandinavian mountains.
Very rare breeder in Scotland (about four pairs).
Movements Summer visitor to breeding grounds. Migrates
to southern and south-eastern European coasts in autumn.
In British Isles, rarer as passage bird than Little Stint.

Red-necked Phalarope

Phalaropus lobatus
18–19 cm (7–8 ins)

Identification Small, delicate wader
with fine, needle-like bill. Female has
showy breeding plumage, with white
chin and bright rust-brown band at
sides of neck and breast. Male less
colourful. Winter plumage is grey with
dark on top of head and dark patch through eye. In flight,
shows prominent white wing-bar. Often swims when feeding,
turning abruptly on axis to stir up food from sediment.
Voice Squeaky 'kritt-kritt' or 'pit'.
Habitat Breeds on small lakes and pools. On migration, alone
or in small flocks on open sea, coastal waters or rarely inland.
Breeding range Iceland, Scandinavia, Arctic Russia. Rare in
British Isles: about twenty pairs (mainly in northern Scotland).
Movements Summer visitor to breeding grounds. Migrates
south-east to Persian Gulf and Indian Ocean. Scarce at coasts
of British Isles on migration (mainly storm-driven).
Similar species GREY PHALAROPE★, *Phalaropus fulicarius*, is
larger, with thicker bill. Paler grey in winter than Red-necked.
In British Isles scarce on migration (storm-driven).

Dunlin

Calidris alpina 16–22 cm (6–9 ins)

Identification The most common wader in northern Europe. Bill relatively long and slightly down-curved at tip. In breeding plumage, belly is black. In winter, grey-brown, without black belly patch. Juveniles brown above, with pale feather edges. Forms large flocks; flies in tight formation.

Voice Flight-call a nasal 'krree'. Song, in flight, a purring trill.

Habitat Breeds in tundra, marshes and bogs, coastal grassland and upland moors. Gathers in flocks (sometimes large) on mud flats outside breeding season.

Breeding range Northern and western Europe, north into Arctic and south to British Isles. Main numbers in Iceland and northern Russia. In British Isles, about 9,000 pairs, mainly in Scotland and Pennines.

Movements Resident in south of range, summer visitor further north. Winters around coasts of Europe. British Isles have the highest winter populations in Europe (about 750,000 birds).

Sanderling★

Calidris alba 20–21 cm (about 8 ins)

Identification Small, Dunlin-sized wader with straight, black bill and black legs. In breeding plumage, back, neck and upper breast rust-red with darker spots; white below. Very pale in winter plumage, with dark shoulder patch. In flight silver-grey, with bold white wing-bar. Often runs rapidly in and out of waves at the edge of the surf.

Voice Short 'plitt', often repeated in flight.

Habitat Breeds on bare lichen tundra. Outside breeding season, at coast, mostly on sandy shores.

Breeding range High Arctic.

Movements In British Isles, common passage migrant and winter visitor.

Knot*

Calidris canutus 23–25 cm (9–10 ins)

Identification Medium-sized, rather stocky, short-legged wader with short, straight bill. In breeding plumage, rust-brown, with speckled upperparts. In winter, pale grey upperparts, pale below. Wings rather long and narrow. In flight, shows narrow white wing-bars, and grey rump. Gathers in large, dense flocks, which in flight can seem almost cloud-like.

Voice Rather muted 'wutt-wutt'.

Habitat Mainly sandy and muddy shores (winter).

Breeding range High Arctic (Greenland and Canada).

Movements Winter visitor, mainly to north-western European coasts. Mainly British Isles, Netherlands and France. About 90 per cent of European wintering birds (about 300,000) in Britain (notably in the Wash).

Curlew Sandpiper*

Calidris ferruginea 18–23 cm (7–9 ins)

Identification Dunlin-sized, but less dumpy, with longer legs, bill (slightly down-curved) and neck. Breeding plumage brick red (like Knot). In winter plumage, resembles Dunlin, but has paler belly. In flight, shows white wing-bar and white rump.

Voice Flight-call a trilling 'krillee', softer and less nasal than that of Dunlin.

Habitat Breeds in Arctic coastal tundra. On migration, mostly on mud flats, more rarely on inland muddy sites and salt lakes.

Breeding range High Arctic of East Asia.

Movements Regular passage migrant in small numbers on coasts, especially North Sea. Larger flocks in eastern Mediterranean.

Ruff

Philomachus pugnax
male 26–32 cm (10–13 ins)
female 20–25 cm (8–10 ins)

Identification Breeding male has
remarkable ruff of feathers around neck,
and head tufts. This varies in colour and
pattern between individuals. Front of face with naked skin.
Female and non-breeding male plumage dingy grey. Head
small, and neck rather long. In flight, shows narrow wing-bar
and white base to outer tail feathers.
Voice Usually silent. A low 'wek' flight-call.
Habitat Breeds on open bogs, damp meadows and wet
heaths; favours damp meadows with ditches and ponds,
especially near coast. Outside breeding season, common in
flocks (mainly of juveniles) on mud flats.
Breeding range Mainly north-eastern Europe (Finland
holds about 50,000 pairs). Also Norway, Sweden, Denmark,
northern Germany and Holland. Rare breeder in Britain
(about five females each year).
Movements Summer visitor to north of range, resident in
south. Migrant to coasts of western and southern Europe.

Oystercatcher

Haematopus ostralegus 40–45 cm (16–18 ins)

Identification Large, black and white wader with long, red,
slightly flattened bill and red legs. Juveniles have pale throat
markings and dark tip to bill. In flight, shows broad white
wing-bar and white rump.
Voice Very loud 'kileep', often repeated. On breeding
grounds, an attractive, piping trill.
Habitat Breeds on sandy and shingle beaches,
and also in some areas at inland lakes
and rivers. Otherwise often in large
flocks on mud flats, and coastal fields.
Breeding range Mainly around coasts
of northern Europe. In British Isles, about
40,000 pairs (increasing).
Movements Summer visitor to north of
range, resident in south. Migrant to coasts of
western and southern Europe.

Avocet
Recurvirostra avosetta 42–46 cm (17–18 ins)

Identification Elegant black and white wader with long, upturned bill and bluish legs. Juveniles have brownish cap and back markings. Legs extend well beyond tail in flight.
Voice Musical 'pleet', repeated when alarmed.
Habitat Breeds on salt marshes and coastal lagoons, at estuaries and shallow inland lakes.
Breeding range North Sea coast (sometimes overwinters), parts of Baltic, Mediterranean, and in steppe region of Austria and Hungary. British population (East Anglian coast) around 500 pairs.
Movements Mainly summer visitor. Winters in Africa, and southern Europe, but also around coasts of northern and western Europe (including southern England).

Black-winged Stilt★
Himantopus himantopus 35–40 cm (14–16 ins)

Identification Slim, black and white wader, with unusually long, red legs. Bill thin, straight and black, somewhat longer than head. In breeding season, has black cap and back of neck, or white cap. Male has glossy green sheen to back. Both sexes have grey head and neck in winter. Juveniles have brownish upperparts. In flight, black wings contrast with white rump, belly and tail, and legs extend far beyond tip of tail.
Voice Calls frequently when alarmed: 'kiepp' or 'kyepp'; also a nasal 'kvit-kvit'.
Habitat Breeds near shallow water in estuaries, on shallow lagoons and salt pans.
Breeding range Mainly southern Europe, but north to northern France, Belgium, Holland.
Movements Winters mainly in sub-Saharan Africa, but also locally around Mediterranean.

Great Skua

Stercorarius skua 53–66 cm (21–26 ins)

Identification Largest and bulkiest of skuas, with short tail. Looks rather like juvenile Herring Gull, but wings more rounded. Wings show flashes of white at base of primaries. Chases other sea birds for food, and also eats fish, birds and eggs. Very aggressive at breeding grounds (will attack people).
Voice Deep 'tuk-tuk'; also 'uk-uk-uk' and 'skeerr'.
Habitat Breeds on coastal moorland. Open sea and coastal waters.
Breeding range North-western Europe: Iceland, Faroes, northern Scotland (about 8,000 pairs).
Movements Summer visitor. Migrates to North Sea and Atlantic in winter.

Arctic Skua

Stercorarius parasiticus
46–67 cm (18–26 ins), includes tail up to 8 cm (up to 3 ins)

Identification The most common European skua. Two colour phases occur, with intermediates. Light phase (more common in north) has whitish underside and dark neck band (sometimes missing). Dark phase (mainly in south) is uniformly dusky brown. Two pointed central tail feathers extend beyond tip of tail. Juvenile has shorter central tail feathers.
Voice Gull-like 'ee-air', often repeated.
Habitat Breeds in open tundra and moorland with low vegetation, usually at the coast, or on grassy islands. Outside breeding season at sea, more often near coast than Long-tailed Skua.
Breeding range Northern Europe and Arctic, south to Scandinavian coasts and northern Britain (about 3,500 pairs).
Movements Passage migrant to winter in Atlantic. Regular off coasts of British Isles, mainly in autumn and spring.

Long-tailed Skua★
Stercorarius longicaudus
35–58 cm (14–23 ins),
includes tail 12–20 cm (5–8 ins)

Identification More delicate than other skuas,
with narrower wings; elegant in flight. Has sharply
defined dark cap, white neck and upper
breast. Tail streamers are longer
than those of Arctic Skuas.
Juvenile has shorter central
tail feathers.
Voice Alarm call a series of short, hard
'kree-epp' calls.
Habitat Breeds on upland heath and
tundra. Outside breeding season, mainly
on open seas, more rarely at coast.
Breeding range Mountains of Scandinavia, Russian Arctic.
Movements Summer visitor to breeding grounds. Winters
in Atlantic. Regularly seen in North Sea (mainly autumn)
and Atlantic coast (mainly spring).

Pomarine Skua★
Stercorarius pomarinus
65–78 cm (26–31 ins), includes tail up to 8 cm (up to 3 ins)

Identification Larger and heavier than Arctic Skua, with
broader wings and heavier bill. Central tail feathers
twisted into a blob. Pale phase and (rarer) dark
phase occur. In juvenile, central tail feathers
hardly visible (tail looks rounded).
Voice 'Gek-gek', or 'yee-ee'.
Habitat Breeds on tundra. Winters
mainly at sea (Atlantic).
Breeding range Arctic Russia.
Movements Summer visitor to
breeding grounds. On passage off
coasts in late autumn and late spring.

Herring Gull
Larus argentatus 55–67 cm (22–26 ins)

Identification The most common large gull. White with pale grey back and wings, and black wing-tips. Bill powerful, yellow with red spot; eyes yellow; feet flesh-pink. In winter, head has brownish streaks. Juveniles speckled brown, with black terminal tail band, gradually attaining full adult plumage in fourth year.

Voice Very vocal. Repeated 'kyow'; alarm call at breeding ground 'ga-ga-ga'.

Habitat Breeds in coastal meadows, dunes, on shingle banks, small islands, rock ledges and even on buildings. Otherwise, usually at coast, but also at inland water and rubbish tips.

Breeding range Mainly coastal areas of north-western Europe. British Isles population is around 200,000 pairs.

Movements Summer visitor to north-east of range; resident and winter visitor further south.

Common Gull
Larus canus 38–44 cm (15–17 ins)

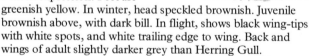

Identification Like a small Herring Gull, but lacks red spot on bill. Rounded white head, relatively narrow, yellow bill and dark eyes, giving rather a meek expression. Feet are greenish yellow. In winter, head speckled brownish. Juvenile brownish above, with dark bill. In flight, shows black wing-tips with white spots, and white trailing edge to wing. Back and wings of adult slightly darker grey than Herring Gull.

Voice Higher and more penetrating than Herring Gull; flight-call nasal 'kyow-kyow'; alarm call 'gleeu-gleeu'.

Habitat Mainly breeds near coast, in colonies in coastal meadows, bog and heath with low vegetation. Mainly coastal outside breeding season, but also on inland waters and fields.

Breeding range North-eastern Europe. Common around Baltic Sea and Scandinavia. Occasional breeder inland in central Europe. In British Isles, about 70,000 pairs.

Movements Summer visitor to north-east of range; resident and winter visitor further south.

Lesser Black-backed Gull
Larus fuscus 52–67 cm (20–26 ins)

Identification Size and shape of Herring Gull, but with dark slate-grey back, and slightly longer wings. Legs yellow. In winter, has streaky head and yellowish pink legs. Juveniles hard to separate from young Herring Gulls, but tend to be darker. Colour on back and wings deepens from grey in south of range to black in Baltic.
Voice Slightly deeper than Herring Gull.
Habitat Breeds on low-lying coasts and islands, usually with higher vegetation than Herring Gull; also on inland moors and bogs. Otherwise, mainly at coasts, but regular at inland lakes. Usually hunts over open sea, but occasionally visits tips.
Breeding range Similar to Herring Gull, but breeds further north (to Arctic) and further south (to coasts of Iberia). British Isles population is around 90,000 pairs.
Movements Summer visitor; migrant and winter visitor from further north.

Great Black-backed Gull
Larus marinus 68–78 cm (27–31 ins)

Identification Our largest gull, with back and wings black. Wings broader than those of Lesser Black-backed Gull. Head large, bill deep, legs flesh-coloured. Juvenile similar to young Herring Gull, but head usually paler. Flight slow, with regular wing-beats and long periods of gliding.
Voice A chuckling 'krau-krau-krau', deeper and slower than Herring Gull; also 'owk'.
Habitat Breeds on rocky and stony coasts, particularly on small rocky islands. Outside breeding season, at coasts and often at rubbish tips.
Breeding range Iceland, Scandinavia, Finland, south to British Isles and north-western France. In British Isles, about 23,000 pairs.
Movements Summer visitor to north-east of range; resident and winter visitor further south.

Black-headed Gull

Larus ridibundus 35–38 cm (14–15 ins)

Identification The most common of the smaller gulls, and the commonest gull inland. Chocolate-brown face mask (not extending down back of neck), with crescent-shaped white mark around eye. Wingtips black, bill and legs dark red. In winter, head white with dark ear-patch. Juveniles speckled brown above with dark trailing edge to wings and dark tip to tail. In flight, the narrow, pointed wings show characteristic white leading edge.

Voice Very vocal: 'kvairr' or 'kverarrr'; also 'ke-ke-ke' and high-pitched 'piee'.

Habitat Breeds in colonies (often large) at reedy lakes, and on small islands and coastal marshes. Very common at coast and on inland waters (and fields) during the winter, even in built-up areas.

Breeding range Throughout Europe, especially in north and east. In British Isles, about 200,000 pairs.

Movements Summer visitor to north-east of range; resident and winter visitor further south.

Mediterranean Gull

Larus melanocephalus 37–40 cm (15–16 ins)

Identification Similar to Black-headed Gull, but has paler and broader wings. In summer, the head is a true black; face has dark mask in winter.

Voice Mostly silent outside breeding season. More nasal than Black-headed Gull.

Habitat Nests in colonies at lagoons and lakes.

Breeding range Scattered from southern Baltic, through central Europe, to northern Mediterranean. Rare breeder in England, with about twelve pairs, mainly in south-east.

Movements Summer visitor to breeding grounds. Winters around Mediterranean, north to Channel.

Little Gull*

Larus minutus 25–27 cm (10–11 ins)

Identification Our smallest gull. Flight tern-like and rather buoyant. Breeding plumage resembles Black-headed Gull, but cap is black and extends further down neck. Also lacks white near eye, and has rounded wing-tips, without black tips. In flight shows slate-black beneath wings, and white trailing edge to wings. Juveniles have dark zigzag pattern on upper wings (see juvenile Kittiwake), and dusky cap.

Voice Soft 'kik-ki-ki' or tern-like 'kyek'.

Habitat Breeds on shallow lakes with rich vegetation, often with Black-headed Gulls. Otherwise, at sea and regularly on large inland lakes.

Breeding range Mainly north-eastern Europe, east of Baltic Sea. A few pairs in the Netherlands and northern Germany.

Movements Mainly summer visitor to breeding areas (resident towards south). Winters around coasts. In British Isles, regular on passage (has bred).

Kittiwake

Rissa tridactyla 38–40 cm (15–16 ins)

Identification Graceful, medium-sized gull. Resembles Common Gull, but wings lack white patches at tips. Legs black, bill yellow. Juveniles have dark zigzag pattern on upper wings (see juvenile Little Gull) and black band across nape.

Voice Flight-call a raw 'ke-ke-ke'; at breeding site a loud, repeated 'kiti-wa-ak'.

Habitat Breeds in colonies on steep cliffs (sometimes on buildings). Otherwise a bird of the open sea.

Breeding range Scattered around coasts of northern and western Europe. In British Isles, on all coasts except much of south and east (total about 545,000 pairs).

Movements Summer visitor to breeding areas. Winters in North Sea and Atlantic.

Common Tern
Sterna hirundo 31–35 cm (12–14 ins)

Identification The most common European tern. Very slim and elegant. Bill bright red, with black tip. Tail streamers do not extend beyond wing-tips when sitting. Winter adults and juveniles have dark bill and whitish forehead. In flight, the dark outer primaries contrast with paler inner primaries.
Voice Very vocal. Flight-call a short, repeated 'kick'. Alarm call 'kee-yah'.
Habitat Breeds in colonies on sandy coasts, in dunes and on islands. Also inland on gravel banks of undisturbed rivers, lakes and ponds.
Breeding range Scattered throughout, most numerous in north and east. In British Isles, about 16,000 pairs.
Movements Summer visitor and passage migrant.

Arctic Tern
Sterna paradisaea 33–35 cm (13–14 ins)

Identification Very similar to Common Tern, and often hard to distinguish in the field. Uniformly red bill, shorter legs and greyer underside. Tail streamers are longer, extending beyond wing-tips when sitting. In flight, shows translucent primaries.
Voice Not quite as harsh as Common Tern, usually a shorter and higher-pitched 'kree-errr'; also a soft 'gik'.
Habitat Breeds entirely on coast, usually with other terns, in large colonies on sand and shingle banks.
Breeding range Arctic region, south through Iceland to Scandinavia, British Isles and southern North Sea. In British Isles, about 46,500 pairs.
Movements Summer visitor. Famous for its long migration route, wintering around Antarctic pack-ice.

Roseate Tern

Sterna dougallii 33–38 cm (13–15 ins)

Identification Paler grey above than previous two species, and with rose tinge to belly in breeding season. Tail streamers extend well beyond wing-tips when sitting, like Arctic, but legs are longer. Bill only usually red towards base.
Voice Most frequent call is chu-vee'; also 'aaak'.
Habitat Islands and shallow, sheltered coasts.
Breeding range An endangered species in Europe. About eighty pairs in France (Brittany). In British Isles, about 500 pairs, mostly in Ireland.
Movements Summer visitor. Winters along coast of West Africa.

Sandwich Tern

Sterna sandvicensis 36–41 cm (14–16 ins)

Identification Relatively large tern, with long, black, yellow-tipped bill, and shaggy crest on back of head. In winter, has white forehead. Slim and narrow-winged in flight, with deep wing-strokes.
Voice Vocal. Shrill, hard 'kjirreck'. Alarm call is a short, sharp 'krik'.
Habitat Exclusively coastal; breeds in colonies on sand and shingle banks, islands, peninsulas, or inaccessible spits. Outside breeding season, in coastal waters.
Breeding range Scattered around coasts of Europe. In British Isles, about 14,500 pairs.
Movements Summer visitor. Migrates to coasts of Africa for winter.

Caspian Tern*
Sterna caspia
47–54 cm (18–21 ins)

Identification Largest
European tern, almost as
big as Herring Gull,
with very powerful red
bill. Extensive black cap,
streaked pale in winter. Juvenile has light brown markings on
cap and dark brown speckled back. In flight, shows dark
undersides to primaries. Gull-like flight with slow wing-beats,
but wing-strokes more elastic.
Voice Heron-like nasal 'kraa-or' or 'kray-krair'. Various other
grating notes.
Habitat Nests in sometimes large colonies on sandy shores,
small coastal islands and at salt lagoons.
Breeding range Baltic coasts of southern Sweden and
Finland; also Black Sea area and Caspian Sea.
Movements Summer visitor. Winters in Africa. Regular
visitor to southern Baltic and (more rarely) to North Sea.

Whiskered Tern*
Chlidonias hybridus
23–35 cm (9–14 ins)

Identification Slightly larger
than Black Tern, and with notched,
not forked tail. Breeding plumage
silver-grey (on belly too), with black cap and white cheeks.
In winter, red bill turns black and crown is white. Skims
surface but also plunge-dives.
Voice Harsh 'krssh'.
Habitat Marshes and lakes, often in deeper water than
Black Tern.
Breeding range Scattered over Europe, mainly central and
southern Europe, notably Spain and France.
Movements Resident in southern Spain, elsewhere summer
visitor. Winters mainly in West Africa. Vagrant to British Isles,
mostly in May or June.
Similar species GULL-BILLED TERN*, *Gelochelidon nilotica*,
breeds mainly around the Mediterranean and Black Seas (also
small colonies in northern Germany and Denmark). Rather
like Sandwich Tern, but with heavier, shorter bill.

Black Tern*
Chlidonias niger
22–24 cm (9–10 ins)

Identification Small tern, with very dark
plumage (in breeding plumage); head
and upperparts grey-black, wings
light grey above and below. With
forked tail, looks rather like a large,
dark Swallow. In winter, white below, with dark on top of head.
Juveniles similar, but darker above and dark mark on body near
base of wing. Hovers and skims water, taking surface prey.
Voice Flight-call a short 'krek' or 'kik-kik'.
Habitat Breeds on shallow, marshy lakes and ponds. Regular
migrant on wetlands and at coast.
Breeding range Scattered throughout Europe, (stronghold is
in north-eastern Europe). Has bred in British Isles.
Movements Summer visitor to breeding grounds. Passage
migrant to central Africa. British Isles, occasional May-August.
Similar species WHITE-WINGED BLACK TERN*, *Chlidonias
leucopterus*, is similar, but with more contrast in plumage and
whiter rump (also white leading edge to wing), and black
underwing coverts. Rare in British Isles (mainly May–Sept).

Little Tern
Sterna albifrons 22–24 cm (9–10 ins)

Identification Small tern, with white forehead even in
breeding plumage and yellow bill with black tip. Crown
whitish in winter, grading into black at back of head.
Juveniles have brownish crown and upperparts with dark
wavy markings. Wing-beats much quicker than those of other
terns. Hovers frequently, often just before diving.
Voice High-pitched raw 'kirrit', 'kirri-ik' or hard 'gik-gik'.
Habitat Breeds on sand and shingle beaches, flat, rocky
coasts, lagoons and on gentle banks of inland lakes.
Usually in small colonies.
Breeding range
Scattered around
European coasts, north
to Baltic, and further east
into Russia. In British Isles
about 2,800 pairs.
Movements Summer visitor.

Guillemot

Uria aalge 38–45 cm (15–18 ins)

Identification Black and white sea bird with narrow, pointed bill. Sits upright, penguin-style. Often has white eye-ring and narrow stripe behind eye (bridled form). In winter, cheeks, chin and neck white, and has a dark line behind eye.
Voice Grating 'aaarrr', 'uarr', at nesting site.
Habitat Breeds in dense colonies on narrow ledges and small ridges on rocky sea-cliffs. Outside breeding season at sea.
Breeding range Coasts of northern and western Europe. In British Isles, over 1,200,000 birds.
Movements Leaves breeding grounds in August, to return in January.

Black Guillemot

Cepphus grylle 30–32 cm (12–13 ins)

Identification Small sea bird with black plumage and white wing patches; feet bright red. In winter, white beneath, grey above, with pale feather edging. In flight, the white wing-patches are conspicuous.

Voice High-pitched whistle 'ssiii' or 'piiiih'; also repeated 'sist-sist'.
Habitat Breeds in small colonies among rocks at base or on lower slopes of sea cliffs and on small, rocky islands. Outside breeding season, mostly in shallow coastal waters.
Breeding range Coasts of northern Europe. In British Isles, about 40,000 birds.
Movements Resident or partial migrant.

Razorbill

Alca torda 39–43 cm (15–17 ins)

Identification Similar to Guillemot but has larger head, shorter neck and heavier bill. Juveniles with smaller, uniformly black bill; easily confused with juvenile Guillemots, but bill shorter and less pointed.
Voice Grating calls such as 'arrr', 'orrr'.
Habitat Breeds in small groups on steep cliffs, often with Guillemots.
Breeding range Coasts of north-western Europe. In British Isles, about 182,000 birds.
Movements Leaves breeding grounds in July to return in February or March.

Puffin

Fratercula arctica 26–29 cm (10–11 ins)

Identification Clown-like face and unusual, heavy, colourful bill. Dumpy, black and white sea bird with bright red legs and feet. In winter, bill becomes smaller and darker. Flight straight, with rapid wing-beats.
Voice Long growling at nest.
Habitat Nests in colonies in rabbit burrows or digs its own on grassy islands or cliffs.
Breeding range Coasts of northern and north-western Europe. In British Isles, about 940,000 birds.
Movements Summer visitor to breeding sites. Winters at sea (Atlantic, North Sea and western Mediterranean).

Collared Dove
Streptopelia decaocto 31–33 cm (12–13 ins)

Identification Pale, slim, long-tailed dove with dark half-collar at back of neck. Breast flushed pink. Rather hawk-like flight silhouette. Courtship involves steep upward flight, followed by slow descent, accompanied by the nasal flight-call.
Voice Flight-call, especially before landing, a characteristic nasal 'shvair-shvair'. Courtship song a monotonous tri-syllabic 'coo-cooo, coo', accented on second syllable (sometimes causes confusion with Cuckoo, if third syllable omitted).
Habitat Mainly towns and villages, especially where there is an abundance of food, as in parks, zoos, grain stores, farmyards. Often seen at bird tables.
Breeding range Throughout most of Europe, except far north-east (rather patchy in south-western Europe). In British Isles, about 230,000 pairs.
Movements Resident and partial migrant.

Rock Dove (Feral Pigeon)
Columba livia 31–34 cm (12–13 ins)

Identification Very familiar as the Feral Pigeon of towns and cities. Very variable in plumage, from blue-grey (colour of original Rock Dove) to rusty brown or almost pure white. Wild Rock Dove always has white patch on rump.

Voice Cooing 'doo-roo-dooo' as part of courtship display.
Habitat Originally rocky sites and sea-cliffs. Feral Pigeon found in towns and cities.
Breeding range Mainly southern Europe (wild type). In British Isles, about 100,000 pairs, including some wild colonies on cliffs of north-west.

Woodpigeon
Columba palumbus 40–42 cm (16–17 ins)

Identification Large pigeon with white patches on wings and neck, visible in flight. Longer-tailed than Rock Dove/Feral Pigeon. Often form large flocks on fields outside breeding season.
Voice Owl-like 'goo-goo-gu-gooroo-roo'. Also loud wing-clapping when flushed, and in courtship flight.
Habitat Woods, meadows and fields; often in trees at field margins. Increasingly in urban parks, feeding alongside Feral Pigeons.
Breeding range Throughout Europe. In British Isles, about 3,520,000 pairs.
Movements Resident in south and west of range (where numbers swelled in winter by migrants); summer visitor further east.

Turtle Dove
Streptopelia turtur 26–28 cm (10–11 ins)

Identification Our smallest dove, with rather delicate build. Plumage rusty brown, speckled wings and black and white markings at side of neck. Juveniles browner and lacking neck marking. Tail shows black feathers and white margin when spread. Flight rapid with slight rocking motion.
Voice Song a soft, purring 'turrr-turrr'; alarm call a short 'ru'.
Habitat Breeds in wooded country, orchards, and sometimes in well wooded parks and gardens. Prefers warm, dry lowland sites.
Breeding range Throughout much of Europe, except far north and west. Very common in Spain (about 1,000,000 pairs). In British Isles, about 75,000 pairs. Recent decline, perhaps due to droughts in winter quarters.
Movements Summer visitor and passage migrant. Winters in Africa, south of Sahara.

Stock Dove
Columba oenas
32–34 cm (12–13 ins)

Identification Resembles grey Feral
Pigeon, but somewhat slimmer, with
grey rump and thin black wing-bars
(often not prominent). In flight,
distinguished from the larger Woodpigeon
by narrower wings with black margins and
tips, and lack of white wing-patches. Flight straight and rapid.
Voice Alarm call a short 'hru'. Song (heard as early as March)
a quiet 'gooo-roo-oo', accented on first syllable.
Habitat Deciduous and mixed woodland, pine woods and
parks with old standard trees. Also in trees at field margins,
orchards. Nests in holes in trees, and needs open country for
feeding. Outside breeding season, often flocks to fields.
Breeding range Most of Europe, except far north. In British
Isles, about 270,000 pairs.
Movements Resident in west and south of range (numbers
swelled in winter by migrants); summer visitor elsewhere.

Cuckoo
Cuculus canorus 32–34 cm (12–13 ins)

Identification Slim, with long wings and
tail. Most often seen in flight, when has
Kestrel-like shape, but markings more
like Sparrowhawk. Normally grey,
but sometimes red-brown.
Brood-parasite of smaller birds
(commonly Meadow Pipit,
Reed Warbler or Dunnock).
Voice Familiar 'cuc-coo' is territorial song of male,
normally heard from the end of April through July.
Female has a loud, bubbling trill.
Habitat Found from high mountains right down to
coastal dunes, fenland and reed beds. Prefers varied
landscape with plenty of cover.
Breeding range Throughout Europe. In British Isles,
about 20,000 pairs.
Movements Summer visitor. Winters in tropical Africa.

Tawny Owl

Strix aluco 37–39 cm (14.5–15 ins)

Identification Our most common
woodland owl. A medium-sized owl
with large, round head and dark eyes.
There are two colour forms: a bark-
coloured grey form and a red-brown
form (latter is more common in British
Isles). More often heard than seen.
Voice Territorial song of male a
shuddering, tremulous 'hoo' (pause)
'huuu-hu-huhuhuh' heard mainly in early
spring. Female (and sometimes male) has
loud 'ke-wick'.
Habitat Deciduous and mixed woodland,
parks, cemeteries and gardens with old trees.
Breeding range Most of Europe, except far
north. In British Isles, about 20,000 pairs.
Absent from Ireland and also from Isle of Man.
Movements Resident.

Barn Owl

Tyto alba 33–39 cm (13–15 ins)

Identification Medium-sized owl with long legs, black eyes
and no ear-tufts. Conspicuous pale, heart-shaped facial disc.
In flight, shows long, slim wings and very pale underparts.
Usually seen when hunting over fields
or ditches at dawn or dusk.
Voice Very vocal at breeding site.
Snarling and screeching sounds,
such as 'khreehreehreeh'.
Habitat Mainly in open,
cultivated areas; breeds in hollow
trees or church towers, barns and
derelict buildings.
Breeding range Most of Europe,
except far north and north-east.
Commonest in Spain and France.
In British Isles about 5,000 pairs
(declining).
Movements Resident.

Short-eared Owl
Asio flammeus 34–42 cm (13–17 ins)

Identification Medium-sized, long-winged owl, often active by day. Has short 'ear' tufts, often invisible. Plumage light brownish grey. Eyes yellow and surrounded by broad black circles. In flight, appears pale and narrow-winged. Wingtips dark; often glides with wings held in V shape; tail wedge-shaped.

Voice Territorial males have soft 'doo-doo-doo-doo' in spring; female replies with 'tjair-op'. Alarm call at nest is a barking 'kwe'.

Habitat Open country with low vegetation. Moorland, heath, overgrown lake margins, and damp meadows or reed beds.

Breeding range Mainly northern and north-eastern Europe. In British Isles, about 2,000 pairs (almost absent as breeding bird in Ireland).

Movements Summer visitor in north of range; resident and partial migrant further south.

Long-eared Owl
Asio otus 35–37 cm (14–15 ins)

Identification Slim, medium-sized, long-winged owl with orange eyes and long 'ear' tufts. Plumage with tree-bark pattern. Nocturnal and rarely seen.

Voice Male has low 'huh', heard as early as February. Alarm call a barking 'wick' which is repeated. Contact call of young birds is a high-pitched 'tsee'.

Habitat Breeds in coniferous forests and plantations, also in light woodland. In winter, often in communal roosts of over twenty birds.

Breeding range Throughout Europe, except extreme north. In British Isles, about 5,000 pairs.

Movements Resident over most of range; summer visitor in north.

Eagle Owl★

Bubo bubo 60–75 cm (24–30 ins)

Identification Our largest owl. Large head with orange-red eyes and well developed 'ear' tufts. In flight, the wings are long and broad, with rounded tips, face looks pointed and tail short.

Voice Song is a deep, far-carrying 'boo-hoo', at intervals of around eight seconds. Female sometimes replies, at a slightly higher pitch.

Habitat Woodland and open country, often near water. Breeds on cliffs (including coastal), steep slopes and also in quarries.

Breeding range Scattered over most of Europe, except north-west.

Movements Resident.

Snowy Owl★

Nyctea scandiaca 55–65 cm (22–26 ins)

Identification Very large and white (male) or white with black flecks (female). Flies powerfully on rather pointed wings.

Voice Alarm-call rather quacking 'kraik-kraik-kraik'; also a softer 'gor'.

Habitat High Arctic tundra.

Breeding range Iceland, Norway. Has bred in British Isles (Shetland).

Movements Resident and partial migrant.

Little Owl

Athene noctua 21–23 cm (8–9 ins)

Identification Small, short-tailed owl with smooth crown and large yellow eyes. Flight is undulating, rather like a woodpecker. Often active by day. Sits on fence posts or telegraph poles.
Voice Alarm call a loud 'kiu'. Male's territorial song is a drawn out, nasal 'guhg'.
Habitat Open country with trees, copses or hedgerows. Also in meadows and pasture with pollarded willows, orchards and the edges of small, open woods.
Breeding range Scattered over most of Europe, but absent from Scandinavia and north-western Britain. In Britain, about 10,000 pairs (absent from Ireland).
Movements Resident.

Scops Owl★

Otus scops 18–20 cm (7–8 ins)

Identification Small, slim, eared owl, with highly camouflaged plumage. Nocturnal and hard to spot.
Voice Song is a monotonous 'dyoo', repeated every two to three seconds. Both sexes may sing for hours, sometimes in a duet.
Habitat Parks, plantations, orchards, avenues or edges of open broad-leaved woodland, often in towns and villages.
Breeding range Mainly southern and south-eastern Europe.
Movements Summer visitor (resident in southern Spain, southern Italy and parts of Greece). Winters to tropical Africa.

Tengmalm's Owl★
Aegolius funereus 24–26 cm (9–10 ins)

Identification Small owl with a large, round head and distinct, dark-bordered facial discs. Dark brown above with white speckles. Juvenile chocolate-brown with white spots on wings and tail. In flight, wings and tail relatively long, and flight direct (not undulating like Little Owl). Nocturnal and hard to spot.
Voice Alarm call a sharp 'tseeuk'. Song of male is a crescendo of hoots: 'poo-poo-poo-poo-poo'.
Habitat Old coniferous or mixed forest; also mountain birch woods. Breeds in old woodpecker holes.
Breeding range Mainly northern coniferous forest (taiga). Also mountain woodland of Alps and other ranges of central and eastern Europe.
Movements Resident. Occasional emigrations occur.
Similar species PYGMY OWL★, *Glaucidium passerinum*, 16–18 cm (6–7 ins), is the smallest European owl. Small head with low forehead, lacking distinct facial discs. Has a similar range and habitat.

Nightjar
Caprimulgus europaeus 26–28 cm (10–11 ins)

Identification Slim, long-winged and long-tailed nocturnal bird, with flat head and large, dark eyes. Plumage highly camouflaged, with bark-like pattern. Small bill opens wide to reveal large gape, surrounded by bristles. Male has white spots on wing-tips and tail. Rather Cuckoo-like in flight.
Voice Flight-call a liquid 'kuik', or when disturbed a raw 'vack'. Male's song is a continuous two-toned purring like 'errr...orrrr-errr', mainly heard in the evening.
Habitat Heathland and light pine woods on sandy soil. Also in thick forest with clearings or felled areas, and in dunes.

Breeding range Scattered over most of Europe, except far north. Highest population in Spain. In British Isles, about 3,000 pairs (fewer than thirty in Ireland).
Movements Summer visitor. Winters in tropical Africa.

Swift
Apus apus 16–17 cm (6–7 ins)

Identification Blackish plumage with pale chin and neck, and long, sickle-shaped wings. Juveniles have pale brow and paler markings on head. Spends most of its life on the wing, often for weeks at a time outside breeding season. Very sociable. Often fly fast in tightly knit flocks. In summer, may circle to a great height in the evening.
Voice Very vocal. High-pitched shrill 'sriieh'.
Habitat Originally a cliff-nester, but now breeds mainly in buildings such as church towers, chimneys and tower blocks. Very common, especially in towns.
Breeding range Most of Europe. In British Isles, about 100,000 pairs.
Movements Summer visitor.

Alpine Swift★
Apus melba 20–22 cm (8–9 ins)

Identification Larger and paler than Swift, with white underside and brown breast-band. Beats wings more slowly, and often glides with wings held low.
Voice Loud, trilling call 'rit-rit-rit-trirr...', rising and falling, with the individual syllables distinguishable.
Habitat Mountains and high rock faces, on rocky coasts and, more rarely, on tall buildings.
Breeding range Mainly a Mediterranean species. Rare breeder in Austria, Switzerland and southern Germany.
Movements Summer visitor. Rare vagrant to British Isles.

Kingfisher
Alcedo atthis 15–17 cm (6–7 ins)

Identification Bright blue above, with rapid flight, low and straight over the water. Easily overlooked when sitting quietly near the bank, and most often seen in flight.

Voice Flight-call a high-pitched 'tieht', 'tii-tee', often repeated.

Habitat Clear streams, lakes and rivers with steep banks in the vicinity (for nest tunnel). Outside breeding season on rivers, lakes and ponds, and also at the coast.

Breeding range Most of Europe, except far north. In British Isles, about 6,000 pairs.

Movements Resident and partial migrant in western and central Europe. Summer visitor in north-east of range (avoids hard winters).

Bee-eater★
Merops apiaster
27–29 cm (11–12 ins)

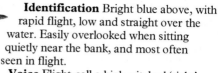

Identification Very colourful and attractive, with pointed wings and long central tail feathers (lacking in juveniles). Flight buoyant, with rapid, deep wing-beats and frequent glides. Hunts insects including bees, wasps, bumblebees and hornets; also butterflies, beetles and flies.

Voice Flight-call is a liquid 'rruip', often repeated several times; territorial call 'grair'; alarm call 'quit-quit-quit'.

Habitat Warm, dry country with good supply of large insects. Breeds on steep river banks, sandy quarries and the like.

Breeding range Mediterranean region and further inland north of Black Sea. North to Austria, Hungary, southern Czech Republic and Slovakia.

Movements Winters in sub-Saharan Africa.

Roller★

Coracias garrulus 30–32 cm (12–13 ins)

Identification Like a bright blue and chestnut crow. Sits in exposed position such as on a pole, telephone wire or branch, waiting for insects, normally taken on the ground.
Voice Raw, hard 'rak-rak-rak' or 'krah'. Also chatters.
Habitat Light woodland with old trees (hole-nester), especially oak or pine; also in tree-lined avenues, isolated trees in fields and in parks. Also nests in steep river banks, cliffs or old walls.
Breeding range Mediterranean region, and further inland in north-eastern central Europe (north to eastern Baltic). Very rare in Austria.
Movements Summer visitor. Winters in tropical Africa. Rare vagrant to British Isles.

Hoopoe★

Upupa epops 26–28 cm (10–11 ins)

Identification Flight-pattern unique and rather floppy, showing contrasting black and white barred wings and tail. Can be hard to spot on the ground. Fan-like erectile crest. Long, curved bill.
Voice Raw, scratching territorial call. Song is a soft, but far-carrying 'poo-poo-poo'.
Habitat Warm, dry, open country, especially cultivated areas, such as vineyards, light woodland, parks, orchards and pasture. Nests in holes in old trees, or in crevices in rocks and walls.
Breeding range Much of continental Europe, north to Channel and Baltic.
Movements Rare but regular spring visitor to Britain (has bred).

Green Woodpecker
Picus viridis 31–33 cm (12–13 ins)

Identification Large woodpecker with
green and yellow plumage and a bright red
crown. Male has red moustache with black
edging, black in female. Juveniles are heavily
barred below, with less intense red on head.
Shows conspicuous yellow rump in flight.
Voice Flight-call (and near nest) a hard
'kjek' or 'kjook'. Laughing territorial song,
'klee-klee-klee-klee-klee', carries over long
distance. Drums only very rarely, and weakly.
Habitat Broad-leaved and mixed woodland,
in copses in fields, orchards, parks and gardens with old trees.
Fondness for ant-rich pasture.
Breeding range Most of Europe, except far north and north-
west. In Britain, about 15,000 pairs (absent from Ireland).
Movements Resident.

Grey-headed Woodpecker⋆
Picus canus 25–26 cm (about 10 ins)

Identification Somewhat smaller than Green Woodpecker,
with greyer head and neck, and
narrower moustache stripe. Male has
red on forehead and front of crown;
female lacks red.
Voice Call 'kju' or 'kjik'. Song of
male (rarely female) is a melancholy
series of descending whistling notes.
Drums in winter and spring, in short,
rather weak bursts.
Habitat Open broad-leaved and mixed woodland;
also in thickets, parks and orchards, and in coniferous
woods to about 1,300 m (4,200 ft).
Breeding range Mainly central, south-eastern and north-
eastern Europe, north to southern Scandinavia. Germany and
Romania have good numbers.
Movements Resident.

Black Woodpecker*
Dryocopus martius
45–47 cm (17–18 ins)

Identification Black, almost crow-sized woodpecker, with powerful, pale bill. Male has red cap, female's cap is red only at back. Flies fairly straight with irregular wing-beats, rather like a Jay.
Voice Flight-call is a far-carrying 'prree-prree-prree', often followed by a descending 'klieerr' on landing. Song in spring 'kwik-wik-wik-wik...', higher pitched than Green's. Drums very loudly, with relatively slow beats.
Habitat Mixed forest with old trees; also northern coniferous forest and beech woods. Nest-hole usually in old beech or pine tree.
Breeding range Mainly central, south-eastern, northern and north-eastern Europe. Southern outposts in Spain, Italy and Greece.
Movements Resident and partial migrant.

Great Spotted Woodpecker
Dendrocopus major 21–23 cm (8–9 ins)

Identification Our most common woodpecker. Black and white plumage, with white shoulder patches; lower tail coverts bright red, flanks unstreaked. Male has red patch at back of head; juveniles have red crown. Flight undulating.
Voice Metallic 'kick', repeated as alarm-call. Most rapid drumming of all woodpeckers. Drums on hollow trees, dry branches, posts.
Habitat Woodland, copses, parks, gardens.
Breeding range Most of Europe. In Britain, about 28,000 pairs (absent from Ireland).
Movements Resident.
Similar species SYRIAN WOODPECKER*, *Dendrocopus syriacus*, is same size, but lacks black bar joining moustache to crown. Eastern and south-eastern Europe only.

Middle Spotted Woodpecker★

Dendrocopus medius 20–22 cm (8–9 ins)

Identification Similar to Great Spotted, but smaller and with weaker bill. Striking red cap with no black border. Flanks have dark streaks; belly yellowish, grading into pink on under tail coverts.
Voice Call (less frequent than Great Spotted) a soft 'gik', or 'ge-ge-ge...' Rarely drums. Song is a musical 'gair-gair-gair...'
Habitat Only in lowland areas, mainly in oak-dominated woodland. Also in mixed river-valley woodland, orchards and parks with old trees.
Breeding range Mostly in warm parts of central, eastern and south-eastern Europe. Some in mountains of Spain and Italy.
Movements Resident.
Similar species WHITE-BACKED WOODPECKER★, *Dendrocopus leucotus* 24–26 cm (9–10 ins), is the largest of the pied woodpeckers, heavier than Great Spotted and with longer bill. Lacks white shoulder patch. Scattered, mainly in eastern Europe (but also southern Scandinavia). THREE-TOED WOODPECKER★, *Picoides tridactylus* 21–22 cm (about 8 ins), is black and white with yellow crown. Mainly in northern conifer forests (and mountains of central and south-eastern Europe).

Lesser Spotted Woodpecker

Dendrocopus minor 14–15 cm (about 6 ins)

Identification Smallest European woodpecker, sparrow-sized. Back is black with horizontal white bands; no red on underside. Male has red cap with black margin, female has no red colour at all.
Voice Song is a soft 'kee-kee-kee...', usually heard in spring. Male and female drum (rather long, yet weak).
Habitat Broad-leaved and mixed woodland, damp woods and riverside trees; also in parks with old willows or poplars, and orchards. Sometimes in gardens.
Breeding range Scattered throughout Europe. In Britain, about 5,000 pairs (not Ireland).
Movements Resident.

Wryneck
Jynx torquilla 16–17 cm (6–6.5 ins)

Identification Strange-looking woodpecker relative,
with Nightjar-like bark-coloured plumage
and short bill. Could only be mistaken
for Barred Warbler.
Voice Call a hissing 'gshree'. Song a
monotonous crescendo 'kyee-kyee-kyee...'
sung by both sexes, often as a duet.
Habitat Light broad-leaved woodland,
copses, parks, and orchards. Avoids closed
woodland. Feeds on ground.
Breeding range Scattered over most of
continental Europe. In British Isles, very few
(perhaps five) pairs (Scotland).
Movements Summer visitor. Regular, but
rare, passage migrant to British Isles.

Woodlark
Lullula arborea about 15 cm (6 ins)

Identification Smaller and shorter-tailed than Skylark.
Has pale eye-stripes, meeting at nape, and black and white
markings at the bend of wing. Crest rather small and
rounded, often inconspicuous.
Voice Call a soft, liquid 'did-loee'. Song rather beautiful, made
up of different melancholy phrases such as 'dleedlee-dleedlee-
dleedlee', falling towards the end. Richly varied repertoire.
Sings early in season (from February in Britain).
Habitat Woodland clearings in pine forests or on
wooded heathland. Often nests near Tree Pipit.
Breeding range Scattered throughout Europe, except in
north and north-west. Declined
over much of range;
distribution rather patchy.
In Britain, about 350 pairs
(absent from Ireland).
Movements Summer visitor in
north of range; mainly resident
further south.

Crested Lark★
Galerida cristata
16–18 cm (6–7 ins)

Identification More compact and shorter-tailed than Skylark, with somewhat more powerful legs, and longer slightly decurved bill. Crest more conspicuous. Flight soft and flappy, showing broad wings and yellow-brown outer tail feathers.

Voice Flight-call a musical 'djui'. Song of whistled or twittering phrases, often containing imitations of other species.

Habitat Dry open country, steppe, semi-desert. Also embankments and waste ground.

Breeding range Distribution patchy through most of Europe; absent from northern and north-western Europe.

Movements Resident.

Similar species THEKLA LARK★, *Galerida theklae* about 16 cm (6.5 ins), is almost identical, but has shorter crest and shorter bill. Spain and southern France only. SHORT-TOED LARK★, *Calandrella brachydactyla* about 14 cm (5.5 ins), is smaller, pale and finch-like, lacks crest. Mainly Mediterranean. LESSER SHORT-TOED LARK★, *Calandrella rufescens* 13–14 cm (about 5 ins), is greyer and more streaked than Short-toed Lark. It occurs mainly in Spain and Turkey, in salty steppe country.

Skylark
Alauda arvensis 18–19 cm (about 7 ins)

Identification Common large lark of open country, with camouflaged plumage and small crest. Trailing edges of wings and outer tail feathers white.

Voice Flight-call a pleasant 'chree' or 'chreeoo'. Song, usually in long, vertical song-flight, is a continuous mixture of trills and whistles. Often includes imitations of other birds.

Habitat Open country, especially fields and pasture, meadows and downland.

Breeding range Throughout Europe. In British Isles, about 2,500,000 pairs.

Movements Resident and partial migrant in south and west of range. Summer visitor in north and east.

Shore Lark★
Eremophila alpestris
15–17 cm (6–7 ins)

Identification Sandy grey
above, whitish below. Yellow
and black head markings, less
distinct in winter, especially in
the female. Breeding male has
small black 'horns'. In flight,
slimmer than other larks, and with rather pointed wings.
Voice Flight-call a tinkling 'seet-dit-dit'. Song is a rapid, high-
pitched twitter, in short phrases.
Habitat Breeds in open mountain habitats on dry, stony
plateaux. In winter, on coastal meadows, wasteland and fields.
Breeding range Scandinavian and Balkan mountains.
Movements Summer visitor in north; resident in Balkans.
Winter visitor to North Sea and southern Baltic coasts.
Similar species CALANDRA LARK★, *Melanocorypha calandra*
18–19 cm (about 7 ins), is heavy and finch-like, with black
neck-patch. Resident in southern Europe.

Meadow Pipit
Anthus pratensis about 15 cm (6 ins)

Identification Small, rather featureless,
common bird of open country. Differs
from similar Tree Pipit mainly by voice
and habitat. Breast has less yellow,
and is more delicately streaked.
Flight rather undulating.
Voice When flushed, high-
pitched 'ist'; also a soft 'psip'.
Song an accelerating series
of 'tsip' calls.
Habitat Moorland, wet meadows, heath, dunes and waste
ground; in mountains on meadows up to tree-line.
Breeding range Mainly northern Europe, south to Alps.
In British Isles, about 2,000,000 pairs.
Movements Summer visitor in north of range; resident in
south and west of range, including British Isles.

Tree Pipit
Anthus trivialis about 15 cm (6 ins)

Identification Slim, with yellowish breast and neck, streaked heavily with dark brown. Legs reddish. Slightly larger and paler than Meadow Pipit.

Voice When flushed, 'psee' or 'tsitt', often repeated. Song louder and more musical than Meadow Pipit's, with long Canary-like phrases. Usually sings in parachuting flight from a tree and when returning to the perch.

Habitat Breeds on margins of broad-leaved and coniferous forest, in clearings, and in heathland with scattered trees or bushes. Also found around tree-line in mountains.

Breeding range Scattered over most of Europe except the extreme south. In Britain, about 120,000 pairs (virtually absent from Ireland).

Movements Summer visitor.

Tawny Pipit★
Anthus campestris about 17 cm (6.5 ins)

Identification Larger and slimmer than Tree Pipit, and with longer legs and tail; rather wagtail-like in shape. Plumage sandy and almost unstreaked, with clear eye-stripe. Juveniles streaked above and on breast.

Voice Flight-call 'tshree' or 'psia'. Song is a monotonous, repeated 'tseerluih', in undulating flight.

Habitat Steppe country, dry, open habitats with stony or sandy soils, in clearings in pine forests, vineyards, heathland and in dunes. Also on alpine meadows.

Breeding range Mainly southern and eastern Europe; also scattered in central Europe. Absent from northern and north-western Europe.

Movements Summer visitor.

Rock Pipit
Anthus petrosus
about 17 cm (6.5 ins)

Identification Large and dark,
with long bill and dark legs. Outer
tail feathers are grey.
Voice Call 'weest'. Song, given in
flapping song-flight, resembles that
of Meadow Pipit, but with stronger trill at the end.
Habitat Stony and rocky shorelines.
Breeding range Coasts of northern and western Europe. In
British Isles, about 45,000 pairs.
Movements Resident and partial migrant. Winters regularly
around North Sea and Baltic.
Similar species WATER PIPIT*, *Anthus spinoletta* about 17 cm
(6.5 ins), is a bird of mountain meadows above the tree-line,
Alps and other mountains of central and southern Europe.
Winters north to British Isles.

Pied Wagtail
Motacilla alba about 18 cm (7 ins)

Identification Long,
black tail with white outer
feathers, and long, black
legs. The continental race,
sometimes known as White Wagtail
(*M. alba alba*), has light grey back
and rump. The British race
(*M. alba yarrellii*), has a black
back. Female less contrasted, and
with less black on head. In winter, has white chin and dark
breast-band. Juveniles brown-grey above, without black.
Voice 'Tsick', 'tsilipp', often repeated. Song is a rapid twitter.
Habitat Open country, especially near water. Towns and
villages, farms, gravel pits. Also seen on lakes and rivers,
meadows, fields and wet areas.
Breeding range Throughout Europe. In British Isles, about
430,000 pairs.
Movements Resident and partial migrant in southern and
western Europe, summer visitor to north and east of range.

Yellow Wagtail
Motacilla flava about 17 cm (6.5 ins)

Identification Somewhat smaller and shorter-tailed than Pied
Wagtail. Yellow Wagtail (*M. flava flavissima*), the British race,
has yellow-green upperparts and yellow stripe above eye. Blue-
headed Wagtail (*M. flava flava*), the central European race, has
slate-grey head and white stripe above eye; female rather duller
with somewhat brownish head. There are other
races in northern and eastern Europe, differing
chiefly in head colour.
Voice Flight-call a sharp 'pseep'. Song of
short, chirping elements.
Habitat Breeds on boggy ground, marshes,
heathland, damp meadows and pasture.
Breeding range Throughout Europe,
except Iceland, Ireland and much of
Scotland. In Britain, about
50,000 pairs.
Movements Summer visitor.

Grey Wagtail
Motacilla cinerea 18–19 cm (about 7 ins)

Identification Yellow beneath, like Yellow Wagtail, but has
much longer tail, grey back and dark wings. Male has black
chin; in winter the chin of male, female and juveniles is white.
Voice Sharp 'tseet-tseet'. Song is of high-pitched, twittering
phrases.
Habitat Breeds along fast-flowing streams and shallow rivers,
and at reservoirs and gravel pits. Outside breeding season also
on lakes and ponds.
Breeding range Most of
Europe, except the north
and east. Absent from most
of Scandinavia. In British
Isles, about 56,000 pairs.
Movements Resident.
Summer visitor in north and
east of range.

Sand Martin
Riparia riparia about 12 cm (4.5 ins)

Identification The smallest European martin. Tail is only weakly forked. Brown above and white below, with brown breast-band.

Voice Very vocal. Scratchy 'tshrr' and repeated 'brr-brr-brr'. Song is a series of soft twitters.

Habitat Sandy banks and quarries (tunnel-nester), usually close to water. Flocks in large numbers at reed beds from summer.

Breeding range Throughout Europe, but distribution rather patchy. In British Isles, about 200,000 pairs.

Movements Summer visitor, wintering in tropical Africa.

Crag Martin*
Ptyonoprogne rupestris about 15 cm (6 ins)

Identification Larger and more chunky than Sand Martin, with notched, not forked, tail. Plumage brownish above; no breast-band; dark lower wing coverts contrast with paler flight feathers. Spread tail reveals row of pale spots. Flight rapid and agile. Patrols cliffs in breeding area.

Voice Vocal. Sparrow-like 'dshri', 'trt-trt'. Song chattering, interspersed with calls and trills.

Habitat Breeds on sunny cliffs in the Alps and Mediterranean area (nest is mud half-cup). In winter, also found over water.

Breeding range Mediterranean region, north to the Alps. Rare breeder in southern Germany.

Movements Resident. Mainly summer visitor in north of range.

Swallow

Hirundo rustica 19–22 cm (7.5–8.5 ins)

Identification Slim and elegant, with long tail (includes tail streamers). Metallic blue above, with red-brown chin and forehead. Juveniles less brightly coloured and with shorter tail streamers. Flight rapid and rather more direct than House Martin's. Often feeds at low level.

Voice Flight-call 'vid-vid' or 'tsi-dit', often repeated. Song a pleasant twittering and warbling.

Habitat Open countryside, villages and farms; mountain pastures. May flock in wetlands at migration. Nest is a mud half-cup.

Breeding range Throughout Europe. In British Isles, about 800,000 pairs.

Movements Summer visitor, wintering in Africa.

Similar species RED-RUMPED SWALLOW★, *Hirundo daurica* 16–18 cm (6–7 ins), is slightly smaller, with rusty rump and nape. Summer visitor to Mediterranean region.

House Martin

Delichon urbica about 13 cm (5 ins)

Identification White rump and pure white underside. Smaller and more compact than Swallow, with short, only weakly forked tail. Metallic blue-black above. Flight is more fluttering than Swallow's; often glides. Usually feeds at higher level than Swallow.

Voice Flight-call 'prrt', 'trr-trr'. Song a simple twitter.

Habitat Towns and villages. Also in quarries and in mountains to 2,000 m (6,500 ft). Builds mud nest with entrance hole.

Breeding range Throughout Europe. In British Isles, about 400,000 pairs.

Movements Summer visitor, wintering in tropical Africa.

Great Grey Shrike★
Lanius excubitor about 24 cm (9.5 ins)

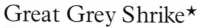

Identification Larger than Red-
backed Shrike, with relatively short
wings, and long, somewhat
graduated tail. Looks black and
white from distance. Juvenile
rather duller, and darker below.
Often sits on a high look-out perch. Flight slow
and undulating; often hovers. Wedges food in tree
branch, or impales it on thorns or barbed wire.
Voice Sharp 'vaird' or 'shrrie', in two or three syllables.
Sometimes a Magpie-like chatter. Song consists of short
metallic or vibrating phrases, and continuous warbling.
Habitat Breeds on moorland, heath; in hedges and orchards.
Breeding range From northern and north-eastern Europe to
south-west. Absent from north-west, south and south-east.
Movements Resident; summer visitor to north-east of range.
In winter, found over most of Europe (at suitable sites).
Similar species LESSER GREY SHRIKE★, *Lanius minor* about
20 cm (8 ins), is smaller, with rather long wings and shorter
tail. Mask extends to forehead. Mainly central, southern and
south-eastern Europe. Summer visitor.

Woodchat Shrike★
Lanius senator about 19 cm (7.5 ins)

Identification Small shrike with rust-red head and
conspicuous white shoulder patches. Blackish above, pure
white below. Female slightly paler, with browner upperparts
and less clearly marked black mask. Juvenile like
young Red-backed, but browner above,
with paler shoulder and rump.
Voice Harsh calls, such as 'kshairr'. Song
varied, with trills, whistles and mimicry.
Habitat Open country: maquis,
vineyards, gardens, orchards and
the like.
Breeding range Mainly
southern Europe, but north to
Poland and southern Germany.
Movements Summer visitor. Annual vagrant to British Isles
(usually in May).

Red-backed Shrike*

Lanius collurio about 17 cm (6.5 ins)

Identification Male has bright red-brown back, grey head with thick black eye-stripe and black tail with white outer feathers at base. Female is red-brown above, pale beneath with crescent-shaped markings. Juvenile has rather scaly markings. Impales prey on thorns (or barbed wire) when plentiful.

Voice Alarm-call 'dshair', 'geck' or a hard 'trrt-trrt'. Song, seldom heard, is a varied warble with short calls, interspersed with imitations of other birds.

Habitat Breeds on heaths, at woodland margins with thorn bushes, and in hedgerows.

Breeding range Throughout Europe, except far north and west. Virtually extinct as breeding species in British Isles (north-west limit of range). May breed again.

Movements Summer visitor, wintering in tropical Africa. In British Isles, regularly seen on passage migration in spring and autumn.

Waxwing*

Bombycilla garrulus about 18 cm (7 ins)

Identification Looks brown from afar, but colourful when close. Starling-like in build and in flight. Female has smaller red wing markings.

Voice Flight-call a buzzing 'sree'. Song a mixture of humming and chattering calls.

Habitat Breeds in open spruce or birch woods with rich undergrowth.

Breeding range North-eastern Scandinavia and Russia.

Movements Summer visitor to breeding grounds. In autumn and winter, mainly to Scandinavia and eastern Europe. Further south and west (as far as Britain) in small numbers; in some years larger numbers occur during 'irruptions'.

iclus about 18 cm (7 ins)

Identification Dumpy, like a large wren in shape. Short tail and powerful legs and feet. Black and brown, with large white bib. Juveniles slate-grey above with dirty white breast and chin. Often sits on a stone in the water, bobbing; flight rapid, direct and low.

Voice Flight-call 'srit'. Song a quiet series of whistles, trills and twitters.

Habitat Fast-flowing clear streams and rivers up to 2,000 m (6,500 ft). In winter, also seen at slower rivers and lakes.

Breeding range Scattered throughout Europe, in suitable habitat. In British Isles, about 20,000 pairs.

Movements Resident and partial migrant.

Wren
Troglodytes troglodytes about 10 cm (4 ins)

Identification One of our most common (and smallest) species. Tiny, with short tail (often cocked). Creeps mouse-like close to the ground or in vegetation or tree roots. Flight is direct, with rapid wing-beats.

Voice Alarm call a loud 'teck-teck-teck' or 'tserrr'. Song is loud and warbling with trills.

Habitat Woods, hedgerows and scrub; also in parks and gardens.

Breeding range Throughout Europe. In British Isles, nearly 10,000,000 pairs.

Movements Resident. Summer visitor in north and east of range.

Dunnock

Prunella modularis about 15 cm (6 ins)

Identification Unobtrusive, rather nondescript, with sparrow-like plumage but Robin-like shape. Head and breast slate grey, flanks with dark streaks. Bill thinner than House Sparrow's.
Voice Alarm-call is a thin 'tseeh'. Song a pleasant warble, gently rising and falling.
Habitat Woodland, parks, cemeteries and gardens.
Breeding range Most of Europe, except the far south. In British Isles, about 2,800,000 pairs.
Movements Resident in south and west of range; summer visitor in north and east.

Alpine Accentor★

Prunella collaris about 18 cm (7 ins)

Identification Larger, squatter and more colourful than a Dunnock. From a distance looks uniform grey-brown, but has rust-red markings on flanks, rather speckled chin and yellowish base to bill. Rather like a lark in flight and behaviour. White tips to tail feathers are visible in flight.
Voice Soft 'trru-trru'. Song a continuous warble with deep trills, somewhat slower than Dunnock's.
Habitat Mountains. Breeds amongst sunny rocks, and on stony alpine grassland. Often around mountain huts and chalets, especially in winter. In summer mostly above about 1,300 m (4,200 ft), in winter lower down.
Breeding range Mountains of central and southern Europe. Widespread in the Alps and Tatra mountains.
Movements Resident and partial migrant. Moves to lower levels in winter.

Cetti's Warbler

Cettia cetti about 14 cm (5.5 ins)

Identification Chestnut and grey warbler, with rather rounded tail. Often heard rather than seen.
Voice Song loud and abrupt: 'chut-chut-chutti-chutti-chutti', from dense cover.
Habitat Lives in damp, overgrown habitats such as fen carr, swamps and ditches.
Breeding range Mainly southern and south-western Europe. Rare breeder in Britain (about 450 pairs), Netherlands, Belgium, and Switzerland. Absent from Ireland.
Movements Resident.

Fan-tailed Warbler★

Cisticola juncidis about 10 cm (4 ins)

Identification Very small with streaked plumage. Fans tail during song-flight (tail has white border).
Voice Call is a hard 'kwit'. Song, usually given in characteristic bouncing and circling flight, is a sharp, high-pitched 'dsip-dsip-dsip...'
Habitat Open grassy areas, often, but not always, near water. Sedge and rush fields.

Breeding range Mainly Mediterranean and southern Europe. Also western and northern France. Very rare breeder in the Netherlands, Belgium and Switzerland.
Movements Resident.

Savi's Warbler
Locustella luscinioides
about 14 cm (5.5 ins)

Identification Tail broad, rounded and graduated. Plumage is unstreaked, rather like Nightingale (but without chestnut on tail); inconspicuous stripe over eye.
Voice Alarm call a short 'tsik'. Song reeling. Shorter, faster and deeper than Grasshopper Warbler's, often beginning with accelerating ticking notes: 'tik tik-tik-tik...'
Habitat Mainly reed beds. Sometimes in rushes and at overgrown lake margins.
Breeding range Mainly central, southern and eastern Europe (notably Hungary and Romania). In Britain, about fifteen pairs (absent from Ireland).
Movements Summer visitor.
Similar species RIVER WARBLER★, *Locustella fluviatilis* about 14 cm (5.5 ins), occurs in eastern Europe (mainly Poland and Hungary), west to Germany. Unstreaked above, but with spotted or streaked breast. Rare vagrant to British Isles.

Grasshopper Warbler
Locustella naevia about 13 cm (5 ins)

Identification Small, olive-brown, streaked above and with narrow, rounded tail. Underside pale, weakly striped. Usually identified by song.
Voice Alarm call 'tschek-tschek'. Song is an even, almost mechanical reeling, often continuing for minutes, by day and at night.
Habitat Thick scrub in marshy areas, damp meadows with tall grass, swampy and river-valley woodland. Also heaths and in dry woodland clearings.
Breeding range A swathe across central and eastern Europe, but absent from much of southern and northern Europe. In British Isles, about 16,000 pairs (rather local).
Movements Summer visitor.

Marsh Warbler
Acrocephalus palustris
about 13 cm (5 ins)

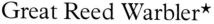

Identification Very like a Reed Warbler,
except for song. More olive-brown above
and not quite so flat-headed.
Voice Alarm-call 'tschak'. Song is loud,
pleasant and very varied, mixed with
squeaking and rattling notes: an
unstructured medley, incorporating much
mimicry. Often sings at night.
Habitat Lush scrub near water, in tall-herb
communities and nettle-beds.
Breeding range Mainly central and north-eastern Europe.
In Britain, fewer than twelve pairs (absent from Ireland).
Movements Summer visitor.

Great Reed Warbler★
Acrocephalus arundinaceus
about 19 cm (7.5 ins)

Identification Largest of the
Acrocephalus warblers (thrush-
sized). Like a Reed Warbler in
plumage, but has long, powerful
bill, more angular head and
conspicuous stripe over eye.
Voice Alarm-call hard 'krek'. Song is
very loud and raw, and with clearly
separated phrases.
Habitat Reed beds, also near ponds, canals
and rivers.
Breeding range Most of Europe, except north and north-
west.
Movements Summer visitor. Vagrant to British Isles.

Sedge Warbler

Acrocephalus schoenobaenus about 13 cm (5 ins)

Identification Small greyish
warbler with clear white stripe over
eye and dark crown. Streaked
above, with unmarked rump.
Voice Alarm-call a hard 'tseck' or
rattling 'karrr'. Song is lively and
scratchy, quite varied, usually
beginning with a short 'trr' and
with long trills.
Habitat Reed beds, marshy scrub
and carr; banks or ditches.
Breeding range Much of northern, central and south-eastern
Europe. In British Isles, about 360,000 pairs.
Movements Summer visitor.
Similar species MOUSTACHED WARBLER*, *Acrocephalus
melanopogon* about 13 cm (5 ins), has more contrasted head
markings and Nightingale-like notes in its song. Scattered in
Mediterranean region, Romania, Hungary and as rare breeder
in eastern Austria. AQUATIC WARBLER*, *Acrocephalus paludicola*
about 13 cm (5 ins), is slightly yellower than Sedge Warbler,
with a darker crown, with a central yellow stripe. Mainly found
in reed beds in north-eastern and central Europe.

Reed Warbler

Acrocephalus scirpaceus about 13 cm (5 ins)

Identification Rather small and drab.
Plumage mainly brown, with white
throat and belly. Skulking behaviour, so
often heard to spot. Bill relatively long.
Voice Alarm call hard 'kra' or 'vet'. Song
similar to Sedge Warbler's, but quieter, less
penetrating, more continuous and faster.
Habitat Mainly reed beds, but also
damp scrub.
Breeding range Most of Europe, except
far north and north-west. In British Isles,
about 60,000 pairs (fewer than fifty in
Ireland); rare in Scotland.
Movements Summer visitor.

Icterine Warbler★

Hippolais icterina about 13 cm (5 ins)

Identification A little larger than Wood Warbler.
Plumage mainly yellowish; posture Reed Warbler-like; long, orange bill. Pale patch on wings.
Voice Call is a musical 'deederoid' or 'taytaydwee'.
Song very varied, with musical whistling calls and much mimicry.
Habitat Broad-leaved and mixed woodland, river-valley woods, parks with undergrowth and gardens.
Breeding range Mainly central, northern and eastern Europe.
Movements Summer visitor. Scarce migrant to British Isles.

Melodious Warbler★

Hippolais polyglotta about 13 cm (5 ins)

Identification Slightly shorter-tailed than Icterine and with shorter wings (lacking pale patch). Only reliably distinguished from Icterine Warbler in the field by song.
Voice Call 'chrett-chrett'.
Song is a prolonged, babbling warble. Some individuals include mimicry.
Habitat Bushy country: olive groves, gardens, plantations; often in willows near water.
Breeding range Replaces Icterine Warbler in southern and western Europe.
Movements Summer visitor. Scarce migrant to British Isles.
Similar species OLIVACEOUS WARBLER★, *Hippolais pallida* about 13 cm (5 ins), is found mainly in south-eastern Europe and eastern Mediterranean region. It resembles a rather grey Reed or Melodious Warbler. Prefers olive groves and scrub.

Garden Warbler

Sylvia borin about 14 cm (5.5 ins)

Identification Plump and rather drab, with no obvious markings. Head rounded, bill relatively short. Grey-brown above, somewhat paler below, with an indistinct eye-stripe, and pale eye-ring.
Voice Call 'vet-vet-vet' or 'tsharr'. Song is soft, with musical Blackbird-like phrases, deeper in tone than Blackcap's.
Habitat Tall scrub, lakeside thickets, bushy woodland margins, woods and parks with rich undergrowth; rarer than Blackcap in gardens.
Breeding range Most of Europe, except south. In British Isles, about 200,000 pairs (about 200 in Ireland).
Movements Summer visitor.

Blackcap

Sylvia atricapilla about 14 cm (5.5 ins)

Identification Grey-brown, with cap black (male), or red-brown (female and juvenile).
Voice Alarm-call a hard 'tak'. Song is very pretty, starting with a soft twitter, and developing into a loud, clear fluting phrase (high-pitched towards the end).
Habitat Open broad-leaved and coniferous woodland, plantations, parks and gardens.
Breeding range Most of Europe except far north. In British Isles, about 800,000 pairs.
Movements Resident in south and west of range; summer visitor further north and east (both in British Isles).

Whitethroat
Sylvia communis about 14 cm (5.5 ins)

Identification Lively warbler with white
throat, grey head and back, and chestnut
wings. Relatively long tail with white outer
feathers. Narrow, white eye-ring. Female
drabber, with brownish head.
Voice Alarm-call 'voit-voit-vit-vit', also
repeated 'tsheck'. Song rather rushed
warble, from bush or in short song-flight.
Habitat Scrub, hedgerows, embankments, woodland edges.
Breeding range Throughout Europe, except far north. In
British Isles, about 780,000 pairs.
Movements Summer visitor.
Similar species SPECTACLED WARBLER★, *Sylvia conspicillata*
about 12 cm (5 ins), looks like a smaller version of the
Whitethroat. It lives in scrub, mainly in southern Iberia,
southern France and Italy.

Dartford Warbler
Sylvia undata about 13 cm (5 ins)

Identification Small, lively warbler, with dark plumage.
Slate-blue above and brown-maroon below. Tail is long and
often held cocked; wings are rather short. Red eye-ring.
Voice Call 'tchrairr'. Song is a short, scratchy warble, from
bush-top or flight.
Habitat Maquis, heath
and scrub.
Breeding range Western
Mediterranean east to Italy;
Spain, Portugal, western
France and southern
England. In Britain, about
900 pairs (not Ireland).
Movements Resident.
Similar species SUBALPINE WARBLER★, *Sylvia cantillans* about
12 cm (4.5 ins), is small, with grey head and back, reddish
chest, red eye-ring and white moustache. Summer visitor to
Mediterranean region only.
SARDINIAN WARBLER★, *Sylvia melanocephala* about 13 cm
(5 ins), is another Mediterranean species (resident). It has a
black head, white throat and red eye-ring.

Lesser Whitethroat
Sylvia curruca about 14 cm (5.5 ins)

Identification Slightly smaller than
Whitethroat, and without chestnut
on wings. Has indistinct mask-like
dark cheeks, contrasting with white
chin, and a relatively short tail.
Voice 'Tjeck', and when alarmed, an
irregularly repeated 'tack'. Song in two parts:
a quiet hurried warble followed by a loud
rattle all on one note. From a distance, only
the second section is audible.
Habitat Scrub, hedgerows. Also found in bushes and hedges
in larger gardens.
Breeding range Much of Europe, except far north, south
and west. In British Isles, about 80,000 pairs (virtually
absent from Ireland).
Movements Summer visitor.

Barred Warbler★
Sylvia nisoria about 15 cm (6 ins)

Identification Large warbler with powerful bill, double white
wing-bar and white tip to tail. Eye is yellow in adult. Female
less barred beneath. Juvenile has
dusky white underside with
indistinct barring, and dark eye.
Voice Alarm-call a rattling 'tr-tr-tr',
or 'tack-tack'. Song similar to
Garden Warbler's, but in shorter
phrases, with typical 'errr' calls.
Habitat Woodland edges, scrub,
hedgerows, juniper heath, overgrown parks with Hawthorn and
Blackthorn.
Breeding range Mainly central, eastern and south-eastern
Europe, west to southern Scandinavia and Germany.
Movements Summer visitor, wintering in East Africa. Scarce
migrant to British Isles (mainly east coast, in autumn).
Similar species ORPHEAN WARBLER★, *Sylvia hortensis* about
15 cm (6 ins), is mainly a Mediterranean species. It has a pale
eye, dark head and white throat. Song is thrush-like.

Chiffchaff
Phylloscopus collybita about 11 cm (4.5 ins)

Identification Very like Willow Warbler, but looks less slim, with shorter wings, and more rounded head. Legs usually dark. Olive-brown above; underside whitish.

Voice Alarm-call 'hweet'. Song is monotonous and irregular repetition of two notes 'chiff-chaff-chiff-chiff-chaff...'

Habitat Broad-leaved and mixed woodland, with plenty of undergrowth, tall scrub, parks and gardens. In mountains to above tree-line.

Breeding range Much of Europe, except far north. In British Isles, over 900,000 pairs.

Movements Resident and partial migrant in south and west of range (including southern British Isles); summer visitor further north. Winters mainly to Mediterranean area.

Willow Warbler
Phylloscopus trochilus about 13 cm (5 ins)

Identification Slim and delicate warbler; best separated from very similar Chiffchaff by song. Somewhat yellower than Chiffchaff, with clearer stripe over eye. Legs normally (but not always) light brown. Juvenile uniform yellowish below.

Voice Alarm call soft 'hoo-eet'. Song is a melancholy descending series of clear notes: 'titi-dje-djoo-dooe-dooi-djoo'.

Habitat Broad-leaved and mixed woodland, clearings, willow scrub, larger parks and gardens.

Breeding range Mainly northern, eastern and central Europe, south to Alps. In British Isles, over 3,000,000 pairs.

Movements Summer visitor.

Wood Warbler
Phylloscopus sibilatrix about 13 cm (5 ins)

Identification Somewhat
larger than Willow Warbler
or the Chiffchaff and with
longer wings. Neck and breast
yellow, contrasting with white belly;
yellow stripe over eye. Lives among
crowns of tall trees.
Voice Alarm-call a soft 'diuh' or
'vit-vit-vit'. Song a descending trill,
beginning 'sip-sip-sip-sipsirrr...', often
including melancholy whistling 'diuh-diuh-diuh-diuh'.
Habitat Tall, open, deciduous or mixed woodland (especially
beech). Also coniferous woodland in east of range. Mountain
woodland in south of range.
Breeding range Widespread, but absent from extreme north
and south of Europe. In Britain, about 17,000 pairs, mainly in
west. There is a small Irish population (around thirty pairs)
which is increasing.
Movements Summer visitor, wintering in Africa.

Bonelli's Warbler★
Phylloscopus bonelli about 11 cm (4.5 ins)

Identification Size of Chiffchaff, but has pale eye-ring and
yellowish or greenish rump, and slightly heavier bill.
Voice Call 'tu-ee'. Song a short trill:
'chee-chee-chee-chee'.
Habitat Broad-leaved or mixed
woodland, Cork Oak groves,
mountain woodland to about
2,000 m (6,500 ft).
Breeding range Mainly
southern Europe, especially
Spain and France.
Movements Summer visitor,
wintering to Africa. Rare vagrant to British Isles.

Goldcrest
Regulus regulus about 9 cm (3.5 ins)

Identification Dumpy and tiny: along with Firecrest, Europe's smallest bird. Olive-green above, with double, white, black-edged wing-bar. Head rather large, bill small and thin. Male has bright yellow crown, edged orange-red; female has light yellow crown. No stripe through or above eye. Juvenile lacks head markings.
Voice High-pitched 'sree-sree-sree-sree'. Song short, very high-pitched, with clear, somewhat deeper, end section: 'sesim-sesim-sesim-sesim-seritete'.
Habitat Mainly coniferous forest or groups of conifers in mixed woodland, parks and gardens.
Breeding range Much of Europe, but restricted to mountain woods in south. In British Isles, about 860,000 pairs.
Movements Resident and partial migrant. Summer visitor in far north and east of range.

Firecrest
Regulus ignicapillus about 9 cm (3.5 ins)

Identification Same size and shape as Goldcrest, but has black stripe through eye and white stripe over eye. Male has orange-red crown, female yellow. Juvenile lacks head markings, but has dark eye-stripe.
Voice Very high-pitched, sharp 'see-seesee'. Song is a high-pitched crescendo of rather similar notes: 'see-see-see-see-see-see-sirrr'.
Habitat Breeds in coniferous forest, but also found in parks, gardens and scrub.
Breeding range Mainly central and southern Europe. In Britain, about fifty pairs (absent from Scotland and Ireland).
Movements Resident and partial migrant. Summer visitor in north of range.

Spotted Flycatcher
Muscicapa striata
about 14 cm (5.5 ins)

Identification Slim and
inconspicuous, with large, dark eyes
and peaked crown. Grey-brown
above, whitish and streaked below.
Juveniles spotted above. Makes
repeated agile forays from perch to catch insects in the air.
Voice Call a sharp 'pst' or 'tseck'. Song is an unremarkable
series of squeaky notes.
Habitat Light broad-leaved and mixed woodland, wooded
pasture, parks and larger gardens. Also dry, open pine forest.
Breeding range Throughout Europe. In British Isles, about
150,000 pairs.
Movements Summer visitor, wintering to tropical Africa.

Pied Flycatcher
Ficedula hypoleuca about 13 cm (5 ins)

Identification Male black or grey-brown
above, white below, with clear white wing-
patch and white spot on forehead. Female
grey-brown above, wing-patch and
underside dirty white. Winter male like
female, but with white forehead.
Voice Alarm-call a sharp 'bit'. Song is an
ascending and descending 'voo-ti-voo-ti-
voo-ti', reminiscent of Redstart's.
Habitat Broad-leaved, coniferous and mixed woodland; in
parks and gardens (will use nest-boxes).
Breeding range Mainly central, north and eastern Europe
(notably Sweden and Finland). In British Isles, about 40,000
pairs, locally in north and west (virtually absent from Ireland).
Movements Summer visitor, wintering to West Africa.
Similar species COLLARED FLYCATCHER*, *Ficedula albicollis*
about 13 cm (5 ins), has white collar, white rump and larger
white wing-patch than Pied Flycatcher. Mainly central and
south-eastern Europe (but also Gotland and Öland). Rare
vagrant to British Isles. SEMI-COLLARED FLYCATCHER*,
Ficedula semitorquata about 13 cm (5 ins), is an endangered
local species of Turkey, Greece and Bulgaria. Its features are
mostly intermediate between those of Pied and Collared.

Red-breasted Flycatcher⋆
Ficedula parva about 12 cm (4.5 ins)

Identification The smallest European flycatcher, grey-brown above, creamy white below, with pale eye-ring and white at base of outer tail feathers. Adult male has orange-red throat bib and greyish head. Female and first-year male lack red bib.
Voice Alarm-call 'doolii', and Wren-like 'tsrrr'.
Song is a descending, whistling phrase, a little
like Willow Warbler's towards the end.
Habitat Breeds in tall deciduous or mixed
woodland. Also in parks in some areas.
Breeding range Mainly central and
eastern Europe, west to Germany.
Movements Summer visitor. Scarce
migrant to Britain (mainly east coast
in autumn).

Nightingale
Luscinia megarhynchos about 17 cm (6.5 ins)

Identification Inconspicuous plumage and retiring habits make it hard to spot. Uniform brown above, except for red-brown tail. Underside slightly paler. Juveniles resemble young Robins, but are larger and have russet tail.
Voice Call 'huit'; alarm call a grating 'karrr'. Song loud and very varied, with warbling and clear fluting phrases, interspersed with deep 'tjook-tjook-tjook', and chirps. Also long crescendo sections, such as 'hiu-hiu-hiu'.
Habitat Broad-leaved or mixed woodland with thick undergrowth, river-valley woodland; maquis.
Breeding range Mainly central and southern Europe, north to British Isles. In British Isles, about 5,500 pairs (absent from Ireland).
Movements Summer visitor, wintering in tropical Africa.
Similar species THRUSH NIGHTINGALE⋆, *Luscinia luscinia* about 17 cm (6.5 ins), replaces Nightingale in northern and eastern Europe. It is greyer and has slightly mottled breast. Song less varied. Rare vagrant to Britain (usually in autumn).

Bluethroat*
Luscinia svecica
about 14 cm (5.5 ins)

Identification Similar to Robin in
shape and size, but with slightly
longer legs. Base of tail rust-red;
pale stripe above the eye. Central
European race (*L. svecica cyanecula*) has
white spot on blue throat; northern European
race (*L. svecica svecica*) has red spot. Female and
winter male have white throat. Juveniles are similar to young
Robins, but with red base of tail.
Voice Alarm-call a hard 'tack'. Song is made up of pure,
sharp calls, together with imitations of other species; often
an accelerating series of bell-like notes at the start.
Habitat Breeds in birch or willow thickets, often by water.
In lowlands, often near swampy lakes and ditches.
Breeding range Mainly northern and eastern Europe, but
scattered southern to central Europe, western France and
northern Spain.
Movements Summer visitor. In British Isles, scarce passage
migrant.

Robin
Erithacus rubecula about 14 cm (5.5 ins)

Identification This familiar garden bird has a rather rounded
shape, relatively long legs, and red breast (sexes similar).
Juvenile lacks red, and is strongly mottled with brown.
Voice Sharp 'tsick', often rapidly repeated; also a high-pitched
'tsee'. Tuneful song, heard from autumn, is a clear
descending series of rippling notes.
Habitat Woodland, especially broad-leaved
woods with rich undergrowth. Also in
parks and gardens.
Breeding range Throughout
Europe. In British Isles, about
6,000,000 pairs.
Movements Resident and partial
migrant. Summer visitor to north
and east of range.

Redstart
Phoenicurus phoenicurus about 14 cm (5.5 ins)

Identification Breeding male has blue-grey crown and back, black face and throat, and orange-chestnut breast and flanks. Female has paler underside and is grey-brown above. Juveniles strongly mottled below.

Voice 'Hooit' or 'hooit-teck-teck'. Song is short, pleasant and Robin-like, usually beginning with 'hooit-tuee-tuee'.

Habitat Broad-leaved, coniferous and mixed woodland, heathland, parks, large gardens and orchards with old trees.

Breeding range Most of Europe. In British Isles, about 150,000 pairs (virtually absent from Ireland).

Movements Summer visitor.

Black Redstart
Phoenicurus ochruros about 14 cm (5.5 ins)

Identification Male has dark, sooty plumage with a pale wing patch, and red rump and tail. Female and juvenile grey-brown.

Voice Alarm-call 'hit-tek-tek'. Song is a short, rapid phrase, starting with 'jirr-ti-ti-ti-ti', and ending with a scratchy sound like sliding gravel.

Habitat On buildings in towns, villages and even in the centres of cities. Original habitat, now mainly in south of range, is mountain rocks and scree to over 3,000 m (10,000 ft).

Breeding range Most of Europe, except far north and east. In British Isles, about 100 pairs, mainly in the south (absent from Ireland).

Movements Resident in south and west of range; summer visitor to north and east.

Stonechat

Saxicola torquata about 13 cm (5 ins)

Identification Male is dark above, with black throat, white half-collar and orange belly. Female and juvenile paler, but still with dark head and ruddy colour below. Often sits at top of bush. Flight low and jerky.

Voice Scratchy 'trat'. Song is a short, hurried phrase with coarse, rattling and whistled notes, sometimes in short, dancing song-flight.

Habitat Open, stony country; heaths, especially those with gorse or broom; also on raised bogs and pasture; to 1,400 m (4,500 ft) in mountains.

Breeding range Mainly southern, central and western Europe. In British Isles, about 20,000 pairs.

Movements Resident and partial migrant; summer visitor in east of range.

Whinchat

Saxicola rubetra about 13 cm (5 ins)

Identification Squat and short-tailed. Male has white stripe above eye, paler in female. Male is dark above, with orange breast.

Voice Hard, very short 'tek-tek' or 'tsek-tsek'. Song is a mixture of short, hurried phrases made up of scratchy, warbling and fluting notes; includes mimicry.

Habitat Open bushy meadows, wasteland. Often near wet habitats, but also on dry heath.

Breeding range Most of Europe, except the extreme south. In British Isles, about 20,000 pairs.

Movements Summer visitor.

Wheatear
Oenanthe oenanthe
15–16 cm (about 6 ins)

Identification Rather active, sturdy bird
with white rump and tail markings, long,
black legs and upright posture. Male has
grey back, black cheeks and wings, and white stripe above eye.
Female and autumn male brownish. Juveniles finely speckled.
Voice Alarm-call 'chak'. Song is a short, rapid, warbling
phrase with hard notes and soft whistles.
Habitat Open stony or rocky country; pasture, moorland and
heath; up to more than 2,000 m (6,500 ft) in mountains.
Breeding range Throughout Europe. In British Isles, about
70,000 pairs.
Movements Summer visitor.
Similar species In southern Europe, BLACK-EARED
WHEATEAR★, *Oenanthe hispanica* about 15 cm (6 ins), is
slimmer, with more white in its tail.
In Iberia, BLACK WHEATEAR★, *Oenanthe leucura* about 18 cm
(7 ins), is larger and all dark, except for white base of its tail.

Rock Thrush★
Monticola saxatilis
17–19 cm (6.5–7.5 ins)

Identification Male rust-red beneath
and on tail, grey-blue above, with
variable white patch on back. Female
and winter male brownish, with large
spots above and mottled yellowish below.
Tail rather short.
Voice Alarm-call is a hard, repeated 'tack' or soft 'jih';
sometimes a Magpie-like chatter. Song is rather a soft, fluting
twitter, often given in parachuting song-flight, with tail spread.
Habitat Mainly mountains, in rocky alpine pasture.
Breeding range Mountains of southern and central Europe.
Movements Summer visitor, wintering in tropical Africa.
Similar species BLUE ROCK THRUSH★, *Monticola solitarius*
18–20 cm (7.5–8.5 ins), is dark blue (male) or brown (female).
Mainly Mediterranean, in mountains and on rocky coasts.
Resident and partial migrant.

Song Thrush

Turdus philomelos about 23 cm (9 ins)

Identification Small thrush with brown upperparts and large, dark eyes. Underside white with small dark spots. Often eats snails, sometimes using a stone as an 'anvil' to break the shell.

Voice Alarm-call a sharp 'tick-tick-tick-tick'. Song loud and variable, with fluting phrases, each repeated two or three times (often more). Sings for long periods from tree-top perch in spring.

Habitat Woodland, copses, parks and gardens with old trees.

Breeding range Most of Europe, except the extreme south. In British Isles, about 1,380,000 pairs.

Movements Resident and winter visitor in south and west of range, summer visitor elsewhere.

Redwing

Turdus iliacus about 21 cm (8 ins)

Identification Slightly smaller and darker than Song Thrush, and with whitish stripe over eye, red-brown flanks, and streaked, not spotted breast. In flight shows the red-brown under wing coverts.

Voice Distinctive 'tsweep' flight-call, audible during autumn migration at night. Alarm-call 'trrt'. Song is a rapid, melancholy descending series of notes, followed by a short twitter.

Habitat Light birch and coniferous forest in the north, up to the edge of tundra. In winter, flocks to fields and open woods, and parks and gardens.

Breeding range Northern and north-eastern Europe. In British Isles, about fifty pairs (mainly in Scotland).

Movements Mainly summer visitor, wintering to central, western and southern Europe.

Mistle Thrush

Turdus viscivorus about 27 cm (10.5 ins)

Identification The largest European
thrush, greyer than Song Thrush and
with longer wings and tail. Grey-
brown above with large spots
below; outer tail feathers
tipped white. Juveniles are
spotted above with pale
markings and whitish neck.

Voice Fight-call a dry 'tzrrr'. Song reminiscent of Blackbird's,
but more melancholy and in shorter similarly-pitched phrases.
Often sings as early as January.

Habitat Broad-leaved and coniferous woodland; also wooded
pasture and large gardens.

Breeding range Throughout Europe, except far north.
In British Isles, about 320,000 pairs.

Movements Resident and winter visitor in west and south
of range, summer visitor in north and east.

Fieldfare

Turdus pilaris 24–26 cm (9–10 ins)

Identification Chestnut back and wings, grey head and rump
and black tail. In flight, shows contrast between black tail, light
grey rump and white lower wing coverts.

Voice Flight-call a loud, raw chatter: 'shak-shak-shak'. Song
fairly quiet warbling and twittering, often given in flight.

Habitat Mountain forests; tundra; also in
tall trees in parks. In winter, flocks to
open fields and farmland.

Breeding range Mainly central
and north-eastern Europe. In
Britain about twenty pairs,
mainly in the north (absent
from Ireland).

Movements Resident and
winter visitor; summer visitor in north
and east of range.

Blackbird
Turdus merula about 25 cm (10 ins)

Identification Very common garden bird, with all black (male) or all brown (female) plumage. Bill and eye-ring of male orange-yellow. Female has weakly speckled breast. Juveniles reddish brown and strongly speckled beneath.

Voice Alarm-call a metallic 'tsink-tsink' and a shrill chatter. Song loud, melodious and fluting, with rather slow phrases (not repeated as in Song Thrush).

Habitat Woods, hedgerows, parks and gardens.

Breeding range Most of Europe, except the far north-east. In British Isles, over 5,000,000 pairs.

Movements Resident and partial migrant. Summer visitor in north-east of range.

Ring Ouzel
Turdus torquatus about 24 cm (9.5 ins)

Identification Similar in size and shape to Blackbird, but with white breast-band (male), slightly longer wings and tail and 'scaly' underside, particularly in winter. Female has fainter breast-band and browner plumage. Juveniles are speckled brown below and on throat.

Voice Alarm call 'tok-tok-tok'; flight-call 'tsreet'. Song of short, repeated, rather rough-toned, fluting phrases.

Habitat Hills, moorland and mountains, alpine coniferous forest. On migration, also in lowland and coastal pasture.

Breeding range Central, eastern and north-eastern Europe, including Alps and other high mountain ranges. In British Isles, about 10,000 pairs (only about 200 in Ireland).

Movements Resident and partial migrant; mainly a summer visitor in north and east of range.

Bearded Tit
Panurus biarmicus about 17 cm (6.5 ins)

Identification Long, cinnamon tail. Male mainly cinnamon-brown with grey head and broad, black moustache, yellow bill and eyes. Female less colourful and without moustache. Juvenile similar to female, but with dark back and sides of tail.
　Voice Flight-call is a very distinctive nasal 'ting', often repeated. Song is short and squeaky.
　Habitat Extensive reed beds.
　Breeding range Scattered throughout Europe, but absent from north and north-east. Common in Netherlands and southern Baltic coastal region. In Britain, about 400 pairs (absent from Ireland).
Movements Resident.

Long-tailed Tit
Aegithalos caudatus 12–14 cm (4.5–5.5 ins)

Identification Very small, but has long, graduated tail, making up more than half of total length. Broad, blackish stripe over eye (but note that the race found in north-eastern Europe has a pure white head). Juvenile has dark cheeks.
Voice Flocks keep up contact calls: 'tserr', 'si-si-si'. Song is a thin trill.
Habitat Woodland with rich undergrowth, often near water; parks and gardens.
Breeding range Throughout Europe, except far north. In British Isles, about 250,000 pairs.
Movements Resident.

Crested Tit
Parus cristatus about 12 cm (4.5 ins)

Identification Brown above, whitish below with cream-coloured flanks and black and white speckled crest. Juveniles have shorter crest.
Voice Alarm-call 'tzee-tzee-gurrr-r'. Song is similar to alarm call, at alternating pitches.
Habitat Pine, spruce and fir forests up to tree-line. Also in small pockets of conifers within broad-leaved woodland.
Breeding range Throughout Europe, except far north and much of south-east. In British Isles, about 900 pairs (Scotland only).
Movements Resident.

Penduline Tit★
Remiz pendulinus about 11 cm (4.5 ins)

Identification Small, with chestnut back and black mask. Female slightly duller; juvenile lacks black mask.
Voice High-pitched, drawn out 'tsiierr'. Song of soft, varied phrases, including call notes.
Habitat River-valley woods with willows and poplars, ponds, rivers and lakes.
Breeding range Mainly eastern Europe and Mediterranean, but scattered northwards to southern Scandinavia.
Movements Resident in Mediterranean; summer visitor elsewhere. Vagrant to British Isles.

Marsh Tit

Parus palustris about 12 cm (4.5 ins)

Identification Small, rather chunky tit
with white cheeks, shiny, black cap and
small, black bib.
Voice Call 'pitchew' or 'psiche-che-che-che...'
Song made up of rattling phrases such as
'tji-tji-tji-tji...' or 'tsivit-tsivit-tsivit...'
Habitat Broad-leaved and mixed
woodland, parks and gardens; usually
in drier habitat than Willow Tit.
Breeding range Most of Europe, except far north, west
and south. In British Isles, about 140,000 pairs (absent
from Ireland).
Movements Resident.
Similar species WILLOW TIT, *Parus montanus* about 12 cm
(4.5 ins), is very similar but has duller black cap, larger black
bib and pale wing panel. Slightly more northern distribution,
into northern Scandinavia. In British Isles, about 60,000 pairs
(absent from Ireland).
SIBERIAN TIT*, *Parus cinctus* about 13 cm (5 ins), is larger,
with brownish crown. It lives in coniferous and birch
woodland in northern Scandinavia and Finland.

Blue Tit

Parus caeruleus about 12 cm (4.5 ins)

Identification Small, compact tit with
blue and yellow plumage. Female slightly
less colourful than male. Juvenile much
paler, with greenish brown upperparts
and yellow cheeks.
Voice Call a nasal 'tsee-tsee-tsee'. Song
is a rather pure-toned 'tseet-see-sirrrrr'.
Habitat Broad-leaved and mixed
woodland, especially oak; parks and
gardens. In winter often feeds among
reeds. Often visits bird tables.
Breeding range Throughout Europe,
except far north. In British Isles, about 4,500,000 pairs.
Movements Resident.

Great Tit

Parus major about 14 cm (5.5 ins)

Identification The largest Euro[ ] with black and white head, yellow[ ] underparts and a broad (male) or narrow (female) black stripe down centre of belly. Juvenile is paler, with yellowish cheeks.
Voice Wide repertoire. Chaffinch-like 'pink' or 'tsi-pink'; alarm-call 'tsher-r-r-r'. Song (variable) is a loud, simple phrase such as 'tee-cher, tee-cher'. Starts singing as early as January.
Habitat Woodland, parks and gardens.
Breeding range Throughout Europe. In British Isles, about 2,000,000 pairs.
Movements Resident.

Coal Tit

Parus ater about 12 cm (4.5 ins)

Identification The smallest European tit, with relatively large head, white cheeks and large white neck patch. Grey above and buff below. Juveniles have yellowish undersides and cheeks.
Voice Contact-call high-pitched, thin 'see' or tsee-tsee-tsee'. Song is of repeated phrases such as 'tsevi-tsevi-tsevi' or 'situi-situi-situi'.
Habitat Coniferous and mixed woods; in parks and gardens with conifers. Also found in broad-leaved woods outside breeding season.
Breeding range Throughout Europe, except far north-east. In British Isles, about 900,000 pairs.
Movements Resident.

ᴺuthatch
Sitta europaea about 14 cm (5.5 ins)

Identification Dumpy and Woodpecker-like,
with short tail and powerful bill. Blue-grey
above, creamy yellow or rusty below.
Scandinavian race has white breast and
belly. Climbs well, up, across and down trees.
Voice Call 'tvit-tvit-tvit'. Song a whistling
'vivivivivi...' or 'peeu-peeu-peeu'.
Habitat Mainly in broad-leaved and mixed
woodland, parks and gardens. Shows fondness
for old oaks.
Breeding range Most of Europe, except extreme north
and north-west. In Britain, about 50,000 pairs (absent
from Ireland).
Movements Resident.
Similar species ROCK NUTHATCH★, *Sitta neumayer* about
15 cm (6 ins), is larger and paler. It lives among rocks and
scrub, mainly in Turkey, Greece and the Balkans.
CORSICAN NUTHATCH★, *Sitta whiteheadi* about 12 cm (4.5 ins),
is endemic to Corsica, where it is the only nuthatch.

Wallcreeper★
Tichodroma muraria about 16 cm (6.5 ins)

Identification Odd-looking bird with long,
rounded wings with red patches and
white spots, long, thin, curved bill and
short tail. Breeding male has
blackish throat and upper breast,
pale in female and winter male.
Flight is butterfly-like.
Voice Fine, high-pitched
whistle: 'tooi'. Song is a series
of scratchy whistles.
Habitat Steep cliffs with clefts and crevices, deep ravines
and gorges. Often at lower altitudes in winter, when
sometimes seen on buildings or ruins.
Breeding range Mountains of central and southern Europe.
Widespread but not common in the Alps.
Movements Resident and partial migrant. Vagrant to
British Isles.

Treecreeper
Certhia familiaris about 13 cm (5 ins)

Identification Woodpecker-like bird with curved bill.
Plumage brown above and white below, with rust-brown rump.
Creeps in spirals up tree trunks.
Voice High-pitched 'srii'. Song is
rather scratchy, ending in a trill.
Habitat Broad-leaved woodland,
mixed woodland, also coniferous
woods (especially in south); parks
and gardens.
Breeding range Mainly central,
northern and eastern Europe.
In British Isles, about 245,000 pairs.
Movements Resident.
Similar species SHORT-TOED TREECREEPER★, *Certhia brachydactyla* about 13 cm (5 ins), is almost identical, but has shorter, louder song. Mainly central and southern Europe.

Snow Finch★
Montifringilla nivalis about 18 cm (7 ins)

Identification Large, with black and white
markings on wings and tail (especially
obvious in flight). Breeding male has grey
head, black bill and black chin. Female is
brownish grey on head with fainter
chin markings.
Voice Sharp, nasal 'pchie'.
Alarm-call a soft,
trilling 'pshrrrt'. Song
a simple twitter.
Habitat Rocky alpine slopes
above tree-line. In winter also seen at cable-car
stations and mountain huts.
Breeding range Mountains of southern Europe,
north to the Alps.
Movements Resident.

Sparrow

mesticus about 15 cm (6 ins)

Identification Familiar small bird of towns. Male has grey cap and black bib; female and juvenile drab grey-brown.
Voice Chirps. Song made up of repeated chirps.
Habitat Houses; villages, towns and farmyards.
Breeding range Throughout Europe. In British Isles, about 6,000,000 pairs.
Movements Resident.
Similar species SPANISH SPARROW★, *Passer hispaniolensis* up to 15 cm (6 in), has chestnut crown and black on belly, flanks and back as well as chin (male). Found in Spain (local); southern Italy (including Sardinia); Greece and Turkey.

Tree Sparrow
Passer montanus about 14 cm (5.5 ins)

Identification Somewhat smaller and slimmer than House Sparrow, and with brighter plumage. Chestnut crown and nape, black spot on white cheek, and small black chin spot. Juvenile has grey-brown head and dark grey chin.
Voice Flight-call a hard 'tek-tek-tek'. Song similar to House Sparrow's but shorter.
Habitat Less dependent on houses and people than House Sparrow. Breeds in open country with hedges, copses and orchards, in parks and at edges of towns and villages.
Breeding range Most of Europe, except far north. In British Isles, about 285,000 pairs.
Movements Resident.
Similar species ROCK SPARROW★, *Petronia petronia* about 15 cm (6 ins), resembles pale female House Sparrow, but has pale white stripe over eye, with brown stripe above. Resident in rocky sites in southern Europe.

Corn Bunting
Miliaria calandra about 18 cm (7 ins)

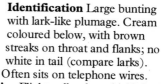

Identification Large bunting with lark-like plumage. Cream coloured below, with brown streaks on throat and flanks; no white in tail (compare larks). Often sits on telephone wires.
Voice Flight-call a sharp 'tick'. Song consists of short, clicking notes which run together into a tinkling final section: 'tik-tik-tik-tik-tik triliriliree'.
Habitat Dry, open cultivated country.
Breeding range Most of Europe, except north and north-east. In Britain, about 20,000 pairs (rather local and decreasing). Rare in Ireland.

Reed Bunting
Emberiza schoeniclus
about 16 cm (6.5 ins)

Identification Breeding male has black head, chin and throat, white collar and white moustache. In winter, head and neck are mottled brown. Female and juvenile have streaky brown plumage with black and white moustache.
Voice Call is 'tsieh'. Song is a short phrase 'tsip-tsip-tete-tsink-tet'.
Habitat Lake and river margins, with reed and sedge beds and damp willow scrub.
Breeding range Most of Europe; scattered in south. In British Isles, about 350,000 pairs.
Movements Resident in central, southern and western Europe; summer visitor in north and east.

Yellowhammer
Emberiza citrinella about 17 cm (6.5 ins)

Identification Slim, yellow-headed bunting with long tail and cinnamon-brown rump. Female and juvenile less yellow, and with dark streaks on head and throat. White outer tail feathers obvious in flight.
Voice Call 'tsik'. Song is a short, melancholy phrase with final syllable at lower pitch: 'tsi-tsi-tsi-tsi-tsi-tsi-tsi-duh' ('little bit of bread and no cheese').
Habitat Heath, open country with hedgerows, copses; bushy woodland margins.
Breeding range Throughout Europe, except extreme south. In British Isles, about 1,400,000 pairs.
Movements Resident; summer visitor in far north, wintering further south in Europe.

Cirl Bunting
Emberiza cirlus about 17 cm (6.5 ins)

Identification Male yellow below with greenish breast-band, and yellow and black markings on head and neck. Female much drabber, rather like female Yellowhammer, but with less yellow and with grey-brown (not chestnut) rump.
Voice Call a high-pitched 'tsiih'. Rattling song somewhat reminiscent of Lesser Whitethroat's, but higher-pitched and more ringing, often all on one note.
Habitat Open, bushy country with isolated trees; vineyards, avenues of trees, gardens.
Breeding range Mainly southern and south-western Europe. In Britain, about 200 pairs in south-western England (absent from Ireland).
Movements Resident.

Ortolan Bunting★

Emberiza hortulana about 17 cm (6.5 ins)

Identification Breeding male has grey-green head, yellow throat and yellow moustache stripe, pale yellow eye-ring and pink bill. Female less green, and with dark streaks on breast. Autumn male resembles female. Juvenile has dark streaks.

Voice Call 'psip'. Song a short, rather melancholy phrase: 'tsri-tsri-tsri-tsri-djer-djer-djer'.

Habitat Cultivated country with orchards, avenues of trees, or scattered trees in fields, woodland margins, often close to wet areas.

Breeding range Scattered throughout Europe, except for north and north-west. Declining over most of its range.

Movements Summer visitor, wintering to tropical Africa. Scarce migrant to British Isles.

Rock Bunting★

Emberiza cia about 16 cm (6 ins)

Identification Male has rust-brown body, ash-grey head with narrow black stripes, and silver-grey throat. Rump rust-brown, tail with white outer feathers. Female has more brown-grey head with dark brown stripes.
Juvenile lightly streaked.

Voice Short 'tsip' or high-pitched 'tsie'. Song rather hurried and high-pitched, reminiscent of Dunnock's.

Habitat Rocky mountainsides. Dry, rocky country and scrub; abandoned vineyards.

Breeding range Mainly southern and central Europe, north to Alps.

Movements Resident and partial migrant.

Snow Bunting

Plectrophenax nivalis 16–17 cm (about 6.5 ins)

Identification Breeding male has white head and underside, black wings with large white patches and black bill. Female has less bright plumage and browner upperparts. Winter male has pale brown back and brownish cap and cheek.

Voice Flight-call a trilling 'tirr'. Song simple and tinkling.

Habitat High mountains and tundra. Regular on north European coasts in winter, on open areas with low vegetation.

Breeding range Arctic tundra and Scandinavian mountains. Iceland. In British Isles, about eighty pairs (Scotland only).

Movements Resident in Iceland and Scotland. Elsewhere mainly summer visitor, wintering to shores of northern and north-western Europe, and further inland in eastern Europe.

Lapland Bunting★

Calcarius lapponicus about 16 cm (6 ins)

Identification Breeding male is streaked above, with black head and face and chestnut nape. In winter, similar to Reed Bunting, but has chestnut patch on wing, framed by two white wing-bars. Bill yellowish.

Voice Flight-call 'prrrt' or 'tew-prrrt'. Song resembles Snow Bunting's but sounds more jerky.

Habitat Mountains and tundra. In winter, on coastal meadows.

Breeding range Arctic tundra and Scandinavian mountains.

Movements Winters around North Sea and Baltic coasts.

Similar species RUSTIC BUNTING★, *Emberiza rustica* about 15 cm (6 ins), resembles Reed Bunting, but has brown markings on breast and flanks. Summer visitor to north-eastern Europe. Vagrant to British Isles.

Serin
Serinus serinus about 11 cm (4.5 ins)

Identification The smallest European finch.
Has very short bill, yellow head and breast
(male), and streaked flanks. Female is
grey-green. Shows yellow rump in flight.
Voice Flight-call high-pitched, trilling
'tir-ri-lillit'. Song is a high-pitched,
jingling twitter.
Habitat Parks, gardens, orchards
and vineyards.
Breeding range Central and southern Europe; absent from
most of northern and north-western Europe. In British Isles,
about five pairs (southern and south-eastern England).
Movements Resident in southern Europe; summer visitor
further north.

Citril Finch★
Serinus citrinella about 12 cm (4.5 ins)

Identification Small finch with
predominantly green and yellow
plumage, but without streaks (male).
Face and underside yellow; nape
and sides of neck grey; two yellow-
green wing-bars; no yellow on tail.
Female darker and weakly streaked above.
Juvenile browner, streaked above and below.
Voice Flight-call high-pitched, nasal 'dit-dit', often rapidly
repeated. Song a lively twitter, similar in tone to Goldfinch's.
Habitat Coniferous mountain forest and alpine meadows.
Breeding range Alps, Pyrenees and other ranges in southern
France and northern Spain, Corsica, Sardinia. A few pairs in
Black Forest.
Movements Resident.

Siskin
Carduelis spinus about 12 cm (4.5 ins)

Identification Very small, greenish, yellow finch
with dark wings and a yellow wing-bar. Male has
black crown and small, black chin patch. Female
grey-green, more heavily streaked and without
black on head. Juvenile browner above and
even more heavily streaked.
Voice Call is a melancholy 'tseelu'.
Song a hurried twitter, with 'tooli' calls
and buzzing.
Habitat Spruce forests and mixed woods,
especially in the mountains, up to the tree-line; conifer
plantations. In winter, often feeds in birch and alder trees,
and also visits bird-tables (likes peanuts).
Breeding range Mainly northern and central Europe.
In British Isles, about 360,000 pairs.
Movements Resident and partial migrant; summer visitor in
north of range.

Goldfinch
Carduelis carduelis about 14 cm (4.5 ins)

Identification Colourful small finch with
black and yellow wings and red face.
Juveniles lack head colours, but do have
the characteristic yellow wing-bars.
Voice High-pitched 'deed-lit'.
Song is a high-pitched, rapid twitter.
Habitat Parks, orchards, hedgerows,
gardens, cultivated fields. Often feeds
on thistles.
Breeding range Most of Europe, except far north.
In British Isles, about 300,000 pairs.
Movements Resident and passage migrant.

Greenfinch

Carduelis chloris about 15 cm (6 ins)

Identification Large, yellow-green or brownish finch. Shows yellow wing-patches, especially in flight. Female mainly grey-green with less yellow on wings and tail. Juvenile heavily streaked.

Voice Calls include 'chup-chup-chup' and nasal 'dzveee'. Song consists of Canary-like trills, with whistles and wheezing notes, often in slow song-flight.

Habitat Mixed woodland, farmland, hedges, parks, orchards and gardens. Common at bird-tables in winter.

Breeding range Most of Europe, except far north. In British Isles, about 700,000 pairs.

Movements Resident (and winter visitor) over most of range; summer visitor in far north of range.

Redpoll

Carduelis flammea 12–13 cm (about 5 ins)

Identification Very small finch with grey-brown, streaked plumage, red forehead and black chin. Breeding male also has pink on breast. Juvenile lacks red.

Voice Flight-call is a rapid, 'dshe-dshe-dshe'. Alarm-call a nasal, drawn-out 'vaiid'. Song is a twitter mixed with buzzing notes and musical whistles.

Habitat Moorland and heath, especially with birch; alder and willow scrub, and lowland coniferous plantations. Also northern and mountain birch and coniferous woodland. Increasingly in gardens.

Breeding range Mainly northern and north-western Europe; also Alps and nearby ranges to north. In British Isles, about 230,000 pairs.

Movements Resident and partial migrant; summer visitor in far north of range.

Twite

Carduelis flavirostris about 14 cm (4.5 ins)

Identification Very similar to female Linnet, but browner and with less white on wings and tail; has yellow-brown, not pale chin. Male has pinkish rump.
Voice Call is a nasal 'chweet'. Song is a rattling twitter, slightly slower than Linnet's.
Habitat Breeds at rocky coasts, mountains, moorland and heaths. In winter, on coastal meadows, salt marshes and stubble-fields; rarer inland.
Breeding range North-western coast of Europe, from Norway to Ireland. In British Isles, about 68,500 pairs.
Movements Resident and partial migrant. Winters in British Isles (mainly northern and eastern coasts), North Sea and Baltic.

Linnet

Carduelis cannabina about 14 cm (4.5 ins)

Identification Mainly brown, active finch. Breeding male has red forehead and breast; duller in winter, with no red on head. Female lacks red, is streaked and dark brown above. Juvenile more heavily streaked. Often forms flocks in open country outside breeding season.
Voice Flight-call rather bouncy 'ge-ge-geg'. Song is rather pretty, beginning with a series of calls, and developing into rapid trills and fluting.
Habitat Open, cultivated country, hedgerows; heathland, parks and gardens. In mountains to tree-line.
Breeding range Most of Europe, except the far north. In British Isles, about 650,000 pairs.
Movements Resident and partial migrant; summer visitor in north and east of range.

Crossbill
Loxia curvirostra
about 17 cm (6.5 ins)

Identification Dumpy, rather large-
headed finch with short, forked tail
and crossed mandibles. Adult male
is brick-red; female olive-green with
yellow rump. Juvenile heavily streaked.
Voice Call 'gip-gip-gip'; also a soft 'tjook'.
Song is rather like Greenfinch's, with
repeated phrases and twitters.
Habitat Coniferous woods, especially spruce, up to tree-line.
Breeding range Scattered across Europe, from coniferous
forests of north-east, to mountain forests further south. In
British Isles, population at least 1,000 pairs (variable).
Movements Resident. Occasionally shows population
irruptions, after which may range widely.
Similar species PARROT CROSSBILL, *Loxia pytyopsittacus*
about 18 cm (7 ins), is slightly larger, with heavier bill. Lives in
north-eastern Europe, but has bred in East Anglia.
SCOTTISH CROSSBILL, *Loxia scotica* about 18 cm (7 ins), has
slightly smaller bill. It breeds in the ancient Scots Pine woods
of Scotland (about 500 pairs).

Hawfinch
Coccothraustes coccothraustes
about 18 cm (7 ins)

Identification Large, heavy-bodied finch
with large head and very large bill. Rather
shy. Female has slightly duller plumage.
Juvenile brownish yellow. Looks thick-set
in flight, and shows pale areas on wings, and white tip to tail.
Voice Sharp 'tsik'. Song (rarely heard) is a jerky, tinkling
mixture of call-like notes.
Habitat Broad-leaved and mixed woodland, parks and
gardens with tall deciduous trees.
Breeding range Scattered through most of Europe, except far
north and north-west. In Britain, about 4,000 pairs, mainly in
south-east (absent from Ireland).
Movements Resident and partial migrant. Summer visitor in
north-east of range.

Bullfinch
Pyrrhula pyrrhula about 16 cm (6 ins)

Identification Male unmistakable, with bright rose-red underparts, blue-grey back, black head and tail and white rump. Female is brown-grey; juvenile brownish, without black cap. Often looks plump, especially in cold weather. White rump prominent in flight.

Voice Call a quiet, plaintive 'dyuh'. Song is a soft, whistling twitter.
Habitat Forest, scrub, plantations, mixed woodland, parks, gardens and orchards.
Breeding range Most of Europe, except far south. In British Isles, about 200,000 pairs.
Movements Resident and winter visitor; summer visitor in far north-east of range.

Chaffinch
Fringilla coelebs 14–16 cm (5.5–6.5 ins)

Identification Our most common finch. Breeding male has blue-grey crown, brown back and pinkish breast. Female is olive-brown above and grey-brown below. In flight, shows white wing-patch and wing-bar, and white outer tail feathers (rump is not white).

Voice Call a loud, short 'pink'. Song is a pleasant, descending phrase, accelerating towards the end.
Habitat Woodland, gardens, parks, scrub; in winter, flocks to farmland.
Breeding range Throughout Europe, except extreme north. In British Isles, about 7,000,000 pairs.
Movements Resident and winter visitor. Summer visitor in north and east of range.

Brambling
Fringilla montifringilla
about 15 cm (6 ins)

Identification Breeding male has black
back, head and bill, with orange breast and
shoulders. In winter, male loses most of black. Female
grey cheeks, black streaks on crown and brown back. Shows
white rump in flight and has less clear wing-bar than Chaffinch.
Voice A rather wheezy 'eeehp'. Song is a soft combination of
Greenfinch-like calls and rattling sounds.
Habitat Northern birch woods and coniferous forests. In
winter, often in large flocks to fields and under beech trees.
Breeding range Scandinavia (as far south as southern
Norway), Finland and northern Russia. Very rare breeder in
Britain, about two pairs, usually in Scotland (not Ireland).
Movements Summer visitor, wintering to most of central,
western and southern Europe.

Starling
Sturnus vulgaris about 21 cm (8 ins)

Identification Familiar dumpy garden
bird with rather long, pointed yellow bill.
In winter, heavily spotted with white and
bill is dark. Breeding plumage has
glossy, green-violet sheen. Juvenile
grey-brown. Flight direct, showing
pointed, triangular wings. Roosts in
large flocks, in trees or reed beds. Often visits bird-tables.
Voice Call 'rrairr' or shrill 'shriin'; alarm-call 'vett-vett'.
Song is very varied, with whistles interspersed with
crackling, snapping and rattling calls, and many imitations
of other birds and sounds.
Habitat Broad-leaved woodland, fields, parks and gardens.
Breeding range Most of Europe, except extreme south and
south-west. In British Isles, about 3,000,000 pairs.
Movements Resident and partial migrant. Summer visitor in
north and east of range.
Similar species SPOTLESS STARLING*, *Sturnus unicolor*
about 21 cm (8 ins), replaces Starling (both present in winter)
in Iberia, Corsica, Sardinia and Sicily. It lacks spots in
breeding plumage.

Golden Oriole
Oriolus oriolus about 24 cm (9.5 ins)

Identification Male is beautiful, with bright yellow body and mainly black wings and tail. Female is green and yellow. Flight undulating (female can be confused with Green Woodpecker in flight).
Voice Call harsh 'kraa', or cat-like mewing. Song is a clear, plaintive, fluting whistle: 'peeloo-peeleoo'.
Habitat Deciduous woods, parks, plantations (often poplar).
Breeding range Throughout Europe except far north and north-west. In Britain, about forty pairs, mainly in south-eastern England (absent from Ireland).
Movements Summer visitor.

Magpie
Pica pica 44–48 cm (17–19 ins)

Identification Large bird with shiny black and white plumage and long, graduated tail. Rather sociable and often seen in small groups.
Voice A chattering 'shak-shak-shak'. Song is low and babbling chatter, with rattling calls and whistles.
Habitat Open country with hedges, pasture, villages, parks and gardens, even in urban areas; avoids dense woodland. In mountains to about 1,500 m (5,000 ft).

Breeding range Throughout Europe. In British Isles, about 800,000 pairs.
Movements Resident.
Similar species AZURE-WINGED MAGPIE★, *Cyanopica cyana* about 35 cm (13–14 ins), is smaller, with buff body, light blue wings and tail and black cap. Found in Iberia only.

Jay
Garrulus glandarius about 34 cm (13.5 ins)

Identification Large colourful crow-relative. Very conspicuous in flight, with black tail, white rump, and white and blue wing-patches. Body buff, with black moustache.
Voice Loud, raw screaming calls. Song a varied, low chatter.
Habitat Mixed woodland, wooded parks and gardens.
Breeding range Most of Europe, except far north. In British Isles, about 170,000 pairs.
Movements Resident.

Siberian Jay★
Perisoreus infaustus
about 28 cm (11 ins)

Identification Smaller than Jay. Pretty grey and pink plumage. Tail is relatively long, with reddish outer feathers.
Voice Calls include 'kook-kook', and mewing notes.
Habitat Northern coniferous and birch forest.
Breeding range North-eastern Europe, south to central Norway and Sweden.
Movements Resident.

Nutcracker★
Nucifraga caryocatactes about 32 cm (13 ins)

Identification Crow-like, with brown, white-spotted plumage. In flight, shows broad, rounded wings, white terminal tail-band, and white under tail-coverts.
Voice Croaking call a nasal 'grairr-grairr', often repeated many times, also 'yek-yek'. Song is a low chatter.
Habitat Mainly coniferous (sometimes mixed) forest. In winter, often seen in Alpine valleys.
Breeding range Southern Scandinavia, north-eastern Europe; also in mountains of central and eastern Europe. Found in the Alps to 2000 m (6,500 ft).
Movements Resident and partial migrant.

Jackdaw
Corvus monedula about 33 cm (13 ins)

Identification Small and crow-like, with mainly black plumage, grey nape and back of head, and pale eye. In winter, often forms flocks with Rooks.
Voice Very vocal. Short, loud 'kya' or 'kyak', often repeated. Song (seldom heard) is a quiet warble with crackling and meowing calls.
Habitat Old, broad-leaved woodland, cliffs, quarries, isolated trees in fields, parks with old trees, churches, castles and ruined buildings. Also breeds in chimneys.
Breeding range Most of Europe, except far north. In British Isles, about 600,000 pairs.
Movements Resident and partial migrant. Summer visitor in far north and east of range.

Chough
Pyrrhocorax pyrrhocorax 38–40 cm (15–16 ins)

Identification Glossy, blue-black plumage, with long, curved, red bill and red legs. Rather acrobatic in flight, showing deeply fingered wings and square tail.
Voice Jackdaw-like calls.
Habitat Rocky sites in mountains; also on rocky coasts in western Europe.
Breeding range Southern Europe, particularly Spain, Greece and Turkey; also Sardinia and Sicily and north-western France. In British Isles, about 1,100 pairs, mainly in Ireland.
Movements Resident.

Alpine Chough★
Pyrrhocorax graculus about 38 cm (15 ins)

Identification Resembles Chough, but has longer tail and smaller, yellow bill. Very agile and acrobatic in flight.
Voice High-pitched whistles and trills.
Habitat High mountains, in steep gullies and at cliffs.
Breeding range Alps, Pyrenees and other mountain ranges of southern Europe.
Movements Resident.

Raven

Corvus corax about 65 cm (26 ins)

Identification Largest black crow, with powerful body and wedge-shaped tail. Very heavy black bill.
Voice Call a deep 'grok', or 'krrooap'.
Habitat Mainly mountains and other rocky sites.
Breeding range Most of Europe. In British Isles, about 10,500 pairs.
Movements Resident.

Rook

Corvus frugilegus about 47 cm (18 ins)

Identification Black, with pale bill and bare, grey bill-base and steep, angled forehead. Belly and thigh feathers tend to be loose, giving trousered effect. Nests colonially and often flocks.
Voice Cawing calls: 'krah' or 'korr'.
Habitat Open, cultivated country; edges of broad-leaved and coniferous woodland, parks, urban areas.
Breeding range Found in a central band across Europe, from France to Black Sea and Baltic. Absent from most of southern Europe and Scandinavia. In British Isles, about 1,375,000 pairs.
Movements Resident and winter visitor; summer visitor in north-eastern Europe.

Carrion Crow

Corvus corone corone about 47 cm (18 ins)

Identification All black, with rather powerful bill. Lacks 'trousers' of Rook. Not colonial, and less sociable than Rook.
Voice Hoarse cawing call, often repeated.
Habitat Open country.
Breeding range Western and central Europe, from Britain, south to Spain. In Britain, about 800,000 pairs (absent from most of Ireland).
Movements Resident.

Hooded Crow

Corvus corone cornix about 47 cm (18 ins)

Identification Belongs to same species as Carrion Crow, but looks very different, with grey body and black face, wings and tail.
Voice Hoarse cawing call, often repeated.
Habitat Open country.
Breeding range Replaces Carrion Crow in northern, eastern and south-eastern Europe, and in north-western Scotland and Ireland. In British Isles, about 450,000 pairs (mainly in Ireland, northern and western Scotland, and Isle of Man).
Movements Resident and partial migrant. Summer visitor in north-east of range.

Further Reading

Boyer, T. & Gooders, J., 1986. *Ducks of Britain & the Northern Hemisphere*. Dragon's World, London & Limpsfield.

Boyer, T. & Hume, R., 1991. *Owls of the World*. Dragon's World, London & Limpsfield.

Brooke, M. & Birkheath, T. (eds), 1991. *The Cambridge Encyclopedia of Ornithology*. Cambridge University Press, Cambridge.

Burton, P. & Boyer, T., 1989. *Birds of Prey of the World*. Dragon's World, London & Limpsfield.

Cramp, S. (chief editor), 1977. *The Birds of the Western Palearctic*. Oxford Univeristy Press, Oxford [7 volumes published, more planned].

Delin, H. & Svensson, L., 1988. *Photographic Guide to the Birds of Britain & Europe*. Hamlyn, London.

Génsbøl, B., 1985. *Birds of Prey of Britains & Europe, North Africa & the Middle East*. HarperCollins, London & Glasgow.

Gibbons, D.W., Reid, J.B. & Chapman, R.A., 1991. *The New Atlas of Breeding Birds in Britain & Ireland: 1988–1991*. T. & A.D. Poyser/Academic Press, London.

Gooders, J., 1994. *Where to watch Birds in Britain & Europe*. Hamlyn, London.

Jonsson, L., 1992. *Birds of Europe with North Africa & the Middle East*. Christopher Helm/A. & C. Black, London.

Lewington, L., Alström, P. & Colston, P., 1991. *A Field Guide to the Rare Birds of Britain & Europe*. HarperCollins, London & Glasgow.

Peterson, R.T., Mountfort, G. & Hollom, P.A.D., 1993. *Birds of Britain & Europe* [5th edition]. HarperCollins, London & Glasgow.

Richards, A., 1988. *Birds of the Tideline*. Dragon's World, London & Limpsfield.

———., 1990. *Seabirds of the Northern Hemisphere*. Dragon's World, London & Limpsfield.

Royal Society for the Protection of Birds, 1993. *Teach Yourself Bird Sounds: 1. Garden Birds; 2. Broad-leaved Woodlands*. R.S.P.B., Sandy, Herts. [Each tape lasts for forty-eight minutes and features over twenty birds with hints on how identify similar songs or calls.

Scott, B., 1994. *Enjoying Wildlife: a guide to the Royal Society for the Protection of Birds' Nature Reserves*. R.S.P.B., Sandy, Herts.

Index

Accentor, Alpine 111
Avocet 73

Bee-eater 95
Bittern 20
Bittern, Little 20
Blackbird 131
Blackcap 117
Bluethroat 125
Brambling 149
Bullfinch 148
Bunting, Cirl 140
Bunting, Corn 139
Bunting, Lapland 142
Bunting, Ortolan 141
Bunting, Reed 139
Bunting, Rock 141
Bunting, Rustic 142
Bunting, Snow 142
Bustard, Great 57
Bustard, Little 57
Buzzard 41
Buzzard, Honey 44
Buzzard, Rough-legged 41

Capercaillie 49
Chaffinch 148
Chiffchaff 120
Chough 153
Chough, Alpine 153
Coot 53
Cormorant 18
Corncrake 52
Crake, Baillon's 54
Crake, Little 55
Crake, Spotted 55
Crane 56
Crossbill 147

Crossbill, Parrot 147
Crossbill, Scottish 147
Crow, Carrion 155
Crow, Hooded 155
Cuckoo 88
Curlew 62
Curlew, Stone 56

Dabchick 15
Dipper 110
Diver, Black-throated 13
Diver, Great Northern 13
Diver, Red-throated 13
Dotterel 60
Dove, Collared 86
Dove, Rock 86
Dove, Stock 88
Dove, Turtle 87
Duck, Long-tailed 36
Duck, Tufted 33
Dunlin 70
Dunnock 111

Eagle, Golden 39
Eagle, Short-toed 40
Eagle, White-tailed 39
Egret, Cattle 21
Egret, Great White 21
Egret, Little 21
Eider 34

Fieldfare 130
Finch, Citril 143
Finch, Snow 137

Firecrest 122
Flamingo, Greater 23
Flycatcher, Collared 123
Flycatcher, Pied 123
Flycatcher, Red-breasted 124
Flycatcher, Semi-collared 123
Flycatcher, Spotted 123
Fulmar 17

Gadwall 30
Gannet 17
Garganey 29
Godwit, Bar-tailed 64
Godwit, Black-tailed 64
Goldcrest 122
Goldeneye 34
Goldfinch 144
Goosander 37
Goose, Barnacle 25
Goose, Bean 27
Goose, Brent 26
Goose, Canada 25
Goose, Greylag 27
Goose, Pink-footed 27
Goose, White-fronted 26
Goshawk 43
Grebe, Black-necked 15
Grebe, Great Crested 14
Grebe, Little 15
Grebe, Red-necked 14

Grebe, Slavonian 15
Greenfinch 145
Greenshank 66
Grouse, Black 49
Grouse, Hazel 50
Grouse, Red 48
Grouse, Willow 48
Guillemot 84
Guillemot, Black 84
Gull, Black-headed 78
Gull, Common 76
Gull, Great Black-backed 77
Gull, Herring 76
Gull, Lesser Black-backed 77
Gull, Little 79
Gull, Mediterranean 78

Harrier, Hen 45
Harrier, Marsh 44
Harrier, Montagu's 45
Hawfinch 147
Hazelhen 50
Heron, Grey 19
Heron, Night 20
Heron, Purple 19
Heron, Squacco 21
Hobby 46
Hoopoe 96

Jackdaw 152
Jay 151
Jay, Siberian 151

Kestrel 47
Kingfisher 95
Kite, Black 42
Kite, Red 42
Kittiwake 79
Knot 712

Lammergeier 38
Lapwing 60
Lark, Calandra 102
Lark, Crested 101
Lark, Lesser Short-toed 101
Lark, Shore 102
Lark, Short-toed 101
Lark, Thekla 101
Linnet 146

Magpie 150
Magpie, Azure-winged 150
Mallard 30
Martin, Crag 106
Martin, House 107
Martin, Sand 106
Merganser, Red-breasted 37
Merlin 47
Moorhen 53

Nightingale 124
Nightingale, Thrush 124
Nightjar 93
Nutcracker 152
Nuthatch 136
Nuthatch, Corsican 136
Nuthatch, Rock 136

Oriole, Golden 150
Osprey 40
Ouzel, Ring 131
Owl, Barn 89
Owl, Eagle 91
Owl, Little 92
Owl, Long-eared 90
Owl, Scops 92
Owl, Short-eared 90
Owl, Snowy 91

Owl, Tawny 89
Owl, Tengmalm's 93
Oystercatcher 72

Partridge, Grey 51
Partridge, Red-legged 51
Peregrine 46
Petrel, Storm 16
Phalarope, Red-necked 69
Pheasant 50
Pigeon, Feral 86
Pintail 31
Pipit, Meadow 102
Pipit, Rock 104
Pipit, Tawny 103
Pipit, Tree 103
Pipit, Water 104
Plover, Golden 61
Plover, Grey 61
Plover, Kentish 59
Plover, Little Ringed 58
Plover, Ringed 58
Pochard 32
Pochard, Red-crested 32
Ptarmigan 48
Puffin 85

Quail 52

Rail, Water 54
Raven 154
Razorbill 85
Redpoll 145
Redshank 65
Redshank, Spotted 65
Redstart 126
Redstart, Black 126
Redwing 129
Robin 125

Roller 96
Rook 154
Ruff 72

Sanderling 70
Sandpiper, Common 66
Sandpiper, Curlew 71
Sandpiper, Green 67
Sandpiper, Purple 68
Sandpiper, Wood 67
Scaup 33
Scoter, Common 35
Scoter, Velvet 35
Serin 143
Shag 18
Shearwater, Manx 16
Shelduck 28
Shoveler 31
Shrike, Great Grey 108
Shrike, Lesser Grey 108
Shrike, Red-backed 109
Shrike, Woodchat 108
Siskin 144
Skua, Arctic 74
Skua, Great 74
Skua, Long-tailed 75
Skua, Pomarine 75
Skylark 101
Smew 36
Snipe 62
Snipe, Jack 62
Sparrow, House 138
Sparrow, Rock 138

Sparrow, Spanish 138
Sparrow, Tree 138
Sparrowhawk 43
Spoonbill 23
Starling 149
Starling, Spotless 149
Stilt, Black-winged 73
Stint, Little 68
Stint, Temminck's 69
Stonechat 127
Stork, Black 22
Stork, White 22
Swallow 107
Swallow, Red-rumped 107
Swan, Bewick's 24
Swan, Mute 24
Swan, Whooper 24
Swift 94
Swift, Alpine 94

Teal 29
Tern, Arctic 80
Tern, Black 83
Tern, Caspian 82
Tern, Common 80
Tern, Gull-billed 82
Tern, Little 83
Tern, Roseate 81
Tern, Sandwich 81
Tern, White-winged Black 83
Terrn, Whiskered 82
Thrush, Blue Rock 128
Thrush, Mistle 130
Thrush, Rock 128
Thrush, Song 129
Tit, Bearded 132
Tit, Blue 134

Tit, Coal 135
Tit, Crested 133
Tit, Great 135
Tit, Long-tailed 132
Tit, Marsh 134
Tit, Penduline 133
Tit, Siberian 134
Tit, Willow 134
Treecreeper 137
Treecreeper, Short-toed 137
Turnstone 59
Twite 146

Vulture, Black 38
Vulture, Cinereous 38
Vulture, Egyptian 38
Vulture, Griffon 38

Wagtail, Blue-headed 105
Wagtail, Grey 105
Wagtail, Pied 104
Wagtail, Yellow 105
Wallcreeper 136
Warbler, Aquatic 115
Warbler, Barred 119
Warbler, Bonelli's 121
Warbler, Cetti's 112
Warbler, Dartford 118
Warbler, Fan-tailed 112
Warbler, Garden 117
Warbler, Grasshopper 113

Warbler, Great Reed 114
Warbler, Icterine 116
Warbler, Marsh 114
Warbler, Melodious 116
Warbler, Moustached 115
Warbler, Olivaceous 116
Warbler, Orphean 119
Warbler, Reed 115
Warbler, River 113
Warbler, Sardinian 118
Warbler, Savi's 113
Warbler, Sedge 115
Warbler, Spectacled 118
Warbler, Subalpine 118
Warbler, Willow 120

Warbler, Wood 121
Waxwing 109
Wheatear 128
Wheatear, Black 128
Wheatear, Black-eared 128
Whimbrel 63
Whinchat 127
Whitethroat 118
Whitethroat, Lesser 119
Wigeon 28
Woodcock 63
Woodlark 100
Woodpecker, Black 98
Woodpecker, Great Spotted 98
Woodpecker, Green 97
Woodpecker, Grey-headed 97
Woodpecker, Lesser Spotted 99

Woodpecker, Middle Spotted 99
Woodpecker, Syrian 98
Woodpecker, Three-toed 99
Woodpecker, White-backed 99
Woodpigeon 87
Wren 110
Wryneck 100

Yellowhammer 140

The Wildlife Trusts

The Wildlife Trusts are pleased to be associated with these excellent, fully illustrated pocket guide books which provide invaluable information on the wildlife of Britain and Europe. For each book sold, a royalty of 1% of the retail price will be be paid by Dragon's World Ltd to the Royal Society for Nature Conservation, the national office of The Wildlife Trusts (RSNC registered charity no. 207238). This nationwide network of wildlife trusts, urban wildlife groups and Wildlife Watch, the junior branch, is working to protect wildlife in town and country throughout the United Kingdom.

If you would like to find out some more, please contact The Wildlife Trusts, The Green, Witham Park, Waterside South, Lincoln, LN5 7JR.